The
Compassionate
Family

Advice and Guidance from
Ayatollah Sayyid Ali Khamenei

Translated by
Alexander Khaleeli and Mona Makki

Collected from the speeches of Ayatollah Sayyid Ali Khamenei

Translated by Alexander Khaleeli and Mona Makki
Edited by Rizwan Rashid and Hina Zehra Rizvi

Special thanks to Sahba Institute for their many efforts in making
this publication available in its original language.

ISBN 978-0-9957589-0-2 (pb)
Second edition published in 2018

Published by
AIM Foundation
info@aimislam.com
www.aimislam.com

Dedicated to the Most Holy and
Compassionate Family, the Ahlulbayt
(peace be upon them)

CONTENTS

PREFACE

The family is the foundation of society, and from it stems new life and a thriving purpose to develop and achieve great things. It is the cornerstone of life and is humanity's greatest social institution.

In Islam, marriage and the formation of a family is regarded as one of the most important objectives for a person to achieve. This importance is demonstrated through the judicial and moral teachings of Islam, which guide us through an array of family issues in order to cater for our spiritual and physical needs.

Today, we live in a world where secularism, individualism and materialism have been aggressively pushed at the human consciousness such that family values are being undermined and eroded. This has resulted in moral decay and other harmful outcomes that prevent the attainment of long-term happiness and stability. Although neglecting family values can allow for a short-lived material fulfilment for some people, the collective prosperity of society cannot be possible without special attention to the family.

This book is our humble contribution to this important subject. It is a collection of advice and antidotes provided by Ayatollah Sayyid Ali Khamenei, a theologian, jurist and statesman who holds the post of being the foremost Islamic authority and head of state of the Islamic Republic of Iran.

Despite all his engagements, Ayatollah Khamenei often conducts the marriage ceremonies of newlyweds, and this book is a collection of some of his words of advice during those sessions.

This book was initially put together by the Sahba Institute in Iran and published in Farsi as a publication entitled 'Khanevade' meaning the Family. It is now available in English to share the Islamic teachings on this subject and to present them as an alternative way to attain happiness as opposed to the current material and secular ideas that are prevalent in our society.

Much thought went into the naming of this book as we felt the literal translation was not sufficient for its new English audience and after many brainstorming sessions we reached the name 'The Compassionate Family' which is inspired by the verse of the Holy Quran:

وَمِنْ آيَاتِهِ أَنْ خَلَقَ لَكُم مِّنْ أَنفُسِكُمْ أَزْوَاجًا لِّتَسْكُنُوا إِلَيْهَا وَجَعَلَ بَيْنَكُم مَّوَدَّةً وَرَحْمَةً إِنَّ فِي ذَلِكَ لَآيَاتٍ لِّقَوْمٍ يَتَفَكَّرُونَ

"And of His signs is that He created for you spouses from among yourselves so that you may find rest in them, and He put between you love and compassion; most surely there are signs in this for a people who reflect."
(Holy Quran 30:21)

We would like to take this opportunity to thank the many people who helped in making this publication a reality and whilst we are only naming a few, there are many others who are unsung heros who assisted us with their time, efforts and donations. They remain the selfless and anonymous helpers whose reward is with God.

We would like to extend special appreciation to Alexander Khaleeli and Mona Makki for their excellent translation of the text, in addition to Rizwan Rashid and Hina Zehra Rizvi for editing and proofreading it.

We would also like to thank the honourable Shaykh Hamza Sodagar for his key role in making this publication happen.

Finally, we thank the Almighty God who blessed us with this opportunity to serve and ask that He accepts this little that we offer in His way.

Sayyid S. Al-Haidari
AIM Foundation
16th February 2017

WITH EVERY MARRIAGE A FAMILY IS BORN

Marriage in Islam is solemnized with a few simple words, yet these words have great consequences. First, two parties will, in reality, be joined and bound together in such a way that they will be closer and more intimate with one another than anyone else in the world. Second, with these words, a new brick in the foundation of society will be laid since the basis of every society is the family.

This is, in fact, the most important outcome of a marriage; namely, that two individual persons become something more—they become a family. Everything else that results from marriage, whether having children or satisfying human needs, is secondary to this fact. First and foremost, marriage means the creation of a new family.

According to the central tenets of Islam, marriage is one of the most important duties for believing men and women. This is because one of the pillars of human existence is the formation of the family unit, which can only be achieved through marriage. This is why we see that all peoples, religions, and cultures believe in some form of marriage. The institution of marriage is not something unique to Islam and each form of marriage is valid for its people. It is for this reason that if, for instance, a non-Muslim couple go on to embrace Islam, their pre-existing marriage is deemed valid; they are still husband and wife and their children are legitimate. We do not say that they need to get married again [in a manner prescribed by Islam]. This is because Islam respects all marriages in other religions and sects, because the principle of marriage, namely an honourable contract between a man and a woman to start a life together, is considered a respectful act in all religions.

Marriage and Sanctity

Normally, a marriage ceremony is a religious ceremony. Christians marry in churches, Jews marry in synagogues, and even though Muslims do not usually marry in mosques, their marriage ceremonies are often conducted on sacred sites; if this is not possible then at least an attempt is made to have them on significant religious days and conducted by religious scholars. Moreover, these religious scholars try to sanctify the occasion with words from the sacred texts. Marriage, therefore, has a religious tone to it and there is an aspect of sanctity that can be found within it.

However, marriage in Islam comes with certain conditions; these conditions not only strengthen the marriage but also direct it towards firm values. What does this mean? It means that by entering the state of marriage we renew our own vows towards God and our religious obligations; we start a family with God in mind. That is why Islam has specified certain acts of worship for every Muslim to perform on their marriage night, including supplications and prayers.

Uninformed individuals assume that marriage is only about fulfilling one's physical desires, even though clearly that is not the case. Fulfilling physical desires is a natural and necessary aspect of human life; not only is there nothing wrong with it, but it is a positive act in and of itself. However, fulfilling these natural desires must be done with the remembrance of God and in the manner that God has prescribed. For example, when we eat food, we begin by invoking the name of God by saying "*bismillāh*" (lit., "with the name of God") and we end by thanking God saying "*al-ḥamdu lillāh*" (lit., "all praise belongs to God); there is no human activity more natural than eating. So when we create a family, we should do this in a way that renews our vows with God, meaning that we remember the promises we have made to God. The first step of this must be to implement them within the institution of marriage. Clearly then, it is very easy to obtain divine reward for an act that also fulfils our natural desires. By simply recognizing that it is the *sunnah* (practice) of our Prophet (ṣ) and by intending to follow this *sunnah*, we can earn divine reward for getting married.

Importance of Marriage in Islam

Marriage is of vital importance in Islam. Even though it is not counted amongst the obligatory acts, it has been recommended to such an extent that God's insistence on it is clearly visible. The reason for this, of course, is that union is a natural desire. As Islam attaches great importance to man's natural desires, it directs these desires towards a healthy fulfilment—namely, marriage. Both women and men have sexual desires, which should not be left free and without limits; such desires are in need of direction and regulation, which are enshrined in marriage. This is emphasized by the following key narration:

$$مَنْ تَزَوَّجَ فَقَدْ أَحْرَزَ نِصْفَ دِينِهِ$$

One who marries, has protected half of his religion[1]

But which half of their religion have they protected? Part of this is that aspect of religion that is threatened by sexual desire. Sexual desire can damage one's religion, affect one's faith, and lead one astray. The only way to prevent this from happening is to fulfil these needs and not suppress them. But how is this to be done? Through the proper medium, of course, and that is marriage. This is the importance of marriage.

Such a relationship is not only found in humans; it exists amongst other creatures and is a means for their reproduction and survival. In other words, we can find something similar to human marriage in plants and animals as well. But because

---

[1] *Biḥār al-anwār*, vol. 100, "Kitāb al-ʿuqūd, abwāb al-nikāḥ, bāb 1 – kirāhah al-ʿuzūbah", ḥadīth no. 14.

man has been granted an intellect and free will, specific rules have been legislated with respect to marriage. These exist to demonstrate the importance of this union between two people and their hearts, a union that is going to create a new element in man's social environment. Such rules regarding marriage are not only found in Islam, but amongst all peoples and creeds. But it is Islam that endeavours to make these arrangements simple and straightforward. It is no wonder then that Islam gives an immense amount of importance to marriage and encourages all people, men and women, to (1) get married, (2) to look after this new social structure created by marriage, and (3) to hold the marriage together; all three of these aspects are highly emphasized in Islam.

The Right Time for Marriage

It is essential that we keep Islam's view of marriage in mind, which strongly encourages the youth to get married. It is wonderful when our young men and women marry at an early age, as soon as they feel the need to do so. We are not insisting that the earlier it happens, the better; rather, we are saying that whenever a young person feels the need to marry, that is the right time for them to do so. Whether that young person is a girl or a boy, you must not let them grow too old.

The Prophet of Islam (ṣ) would encourage people—both girls and boys—not only to marry, but to marry young; of course, it would be out of their own decision and not because they are coerced into it. Today, we need to encourage this same culture of marriage in our societies. Youth should get married while they are still young and full of energy and excitement. This goes against those people who believe that young marriages do not last; in fact, the opposite is actually true. If it is established with care, a young marriage will be both long lasting and healthy, because the couple will share a strong bond with one another.

Putting off marriage until the onset of one's middle age is common practice in Western culture; but, like most other practices prevalent there, it is wrong, it is against man's *fiṭrah* (his God-given innate disposition), it runs counter to the general welfare of mankind, and it actually stems from libertinism and promiscuity. Among the foreign customs that have found their way into our society is the European-inspired idea that a young man needs to have completed his studies and secured a job (and not just any job!) before marriage. This is similar to the idea that a girl should not get married soon after adolescence, but rather must first become a grown woman and experience the world before settling down for marriage. These are irrational customs originating from Europe. The Western practice of getting married later in life is not because they feel that young people do not have sexual desires; in fact, they are completely aware and accepting of the fact that human beings have sexual needs. The problem is that they believe these young individuals can satisfy their needs freely during their youth. But this is precisely what we consider corruption and sin, and it jeopardizes the state of a society as a whole.

This is why the bond of marriage in modern European culture is not a very strong bond. Compare this to traditional families where couples live together for fifty, sixty, or even seventy years, and when one of them dies, the other mourns them for a long time. The foundation of such marriages is affection; these couples are intimate with one another and do not look outside of their married life for the satisfaction of their sexual needs. However, this is not the case with a typical Western couple or family, which lacks a strong foundation, breaks apart easily, and wherein divorce is commonplace. Even when an actual divorce does not take place, one can still speak of a 'divorce' in practice. Without wanting to generalize, many husbands and wives have already spent most of their youth without the need for their partner and then get married after having satisfied their hunger. Even then, they do not restrain themselves to their family life. They are neither here nor there. The only thing that connects them is a room, an apartment, a physical space; it is not a meaningful bond or a spiritual tie that unites them together. Hence, there is nothing familial about their 'families'.

When they get old—and they age quickly (for a sixty year old is a 'senior' according to them)—they no longer enjoy life; but our sixty year olds here count their grandchildren and great grandchildren—now thirty, now thirty-two! This is not the case with many of them because their marriages were not built on love and warmth from the beginning; initially, there was distance, inattentiveness, and an already-satisfied hunger. Of course, I am not saying that all of them are like this, nor am I saying that all of our families here are warm and full of love; I am speaking about what is prevalent in the two societies. What is prevalent in our society is different from what is prevalent in theirs. However, that lifestyle has now infiltrated Muslim lands, but we should know that this is contrary to the teachings of Islam.

Islam says that it is best for young men and women to

marry at an early age—as soon as they start feeling a desire for the opposite gender—and to form a family. What are they waiting for? We have a tradition which states the following:

$$شِرَارُكُمْ عُزَّابُكُم$$

The worst of you are the ʿuzzāb amongst you.[2]

ʿUzzāb means someone who feels the need to marry but has not done so. It applies to both males and females. According to the ḥadīth, they are the worst of people.

Choosing a Spouse

Islam offers us guidance with regard to how to manage a marriage, and this includes guidelines on how to choose a spouse. Whom we choose to be our marriage partner is certainly an important issue. As such, Islam has envisioned a particular set of criteria for choosing a spouse which can be contrasted to a set of 'mindless' (*jāhilī*) criteria, which emphasizes reputation, title, wealth, profession, etc. Those who are infatuated with this world look for worldly qualities in choosing a spouse such as education, wealth, and appearances. Even though these things are naturally attractive and people like them, none of them are necessary ingredients for a happy marriage. What makes someone happy in their marriage is being with a partner who has aptitude, goodness, religion, purity, and honour. These are the ingredients for a lasting and happy marriage.

There is a narration that says that if someone marries a spouse because of their beauty or wealth, it is possible

---

[2] *Biḥār al-anwār*, vol. 100, "Kitāb al-ʿuqūd, abwāb al-nikāḥ, bāb 1 – kirāhah al-ʿuzūbah", ḥadīth no. 31.

for God to take these away. In other words, wealth is a fleeting quality. We see individuals who are at the peak of their wealth and success lose it all at the turn of a moment. Mahathir Mohamad, one of the leaders of an incredibly rich country in Asia with many wealthy citizens, told me that they became poor overnight. It truly was the case. Of course, the kind of poorness he was referring to was related to the politics of nation states; in his words, due to an economic and financial game, thousands of wealthy merchants suddenly found themselves in the dirt. In a single night, the wealth of thousands of people turned into ashes, to be carried off by the wind.

Beauty, whether it relates to man or woman, is much the same as wealth. It is not an enduring quality and it can vanish with any small incident—an injury to the face, a complicated childbirth, an illness, and a thousand other incidents, major or minor, that could materialize for a person. How many individuals do we know who after being known for their beauty lost it after age got the better of them? Therefore, beauty is not a permanent quality. In addition, a person could become accustomed to beauty, and once that occurs, the attraction is lost.

Hence, the attributes that are important in marriage include honour, morality, etiquettes, and religiosity. This is why they say: when you want to choose a spouse—whether a boy or a girl—choose one who is pure and honourable so that God may bless the marriage. The narration that discourages choosing a spouse based on beauty or wealth continues with the following remark: if you seek religion and piety through marriage, God will grant you beauty and wealth. I once asked myself how God can give beauty after having already made a person the way he is. I can understand how a poor person might become wealthy, but how does a person gain beauty? Does God actually transform a person into a beautiful one? What did the Prophet (ṣ) mean when he said that God would give you beauty? Then all of a sudden I realized what it is that *creates* beauty—it is love. When God puts love in someone's heart, even the ugliest face is made beautiful to his eyes. As the poet says:

When you gaze through Majnūn's eyes / you see in Laylā nothing but beauty.[3]

It is said that Layla was unattractive and Majnūn was wretched and deplorable; but what love did was to make them see one another as beautiful and caused them to love each other dearly. Whether this legend is true or not, its story remains.

The point is that when God plants the seed of love in a person, beauty accompanies it. This is because beauty is in the eyes and heart of the beholder. When a man loves a woman, he will find her beautiful even if she is not what is commonly considered to be attractive. Likewise, if a man hates a woman, he will never find her attractive regardless of how pretty she really is. So if marriage is based on God-wariness (*taqwā*) and purity, and the pristine hands of men and women are brought together in wedlock, the love that soon enters the equation will melt away all troubles. Everything will seem sweet and pleasant. As the poet says:

When love comes along, tell burdens to go away[4]

---

[3] A verse by Kamāl al-Dīn (Vahshi) Bafqī.

[4] A verse by Ghina Kashmiri.

Islam says there are only two things you need to consider when getting married. First, the person you choose to marry should be religious, modest, and decent—i.e., her spiritual side should be strong. Second, you should marry on the basis of need. As soon as a man feels like he needs to get married, he should propose to a girl who is modest and decent. Likewise, the girl should take as her husband a modest and decent man. This is sufficient. Pursuing beauty, career, status, family, social convention, or wealth is not what Islam envisions through marriage; in fact, it prohibits this.

It has been narrated that during the time of the Prophet (ṣ), there was a non-Arab man named Juwaybir. He was unbecoming in appearance and possessed no wealth or status within Arabian society. Perhaps there was barely anyone in all of Madinah who was as poor and destitute as he was. Yet the Prophet (ṣ) told him to ask for the hand of the beautiful daughter of one of the richest and noblest families. Juwaybir did not protest and say, "Who am I to ask for her hand in marriage? I am but a poor, unattractive, and worthless person." He did not think this way. He knew that he was a Muslim man and that is what is important. Yes, the girl's father had his faith tested and refused the man. But the girl was strong and devoted to the faith, just like the women who supported this revolution. As soon as she found out that the Prophet (ṣ) had sent this man to propose, she turned to her father and said, "Why did you send him away?" What was this girl thinking? In her mind, he was a Muslim man and she was a Muslim woman, and that was sufficient for them to be a match.

A Muslim is a Muslim's compeer and a believer is a

believer's compeer. This is the Islamic criteria for marriage.

There are individuals who assume that their daughters should only marry someone who is at the same level as her. When they are asked what they mean by 'level', they say, for example, "If we are at a certain level of income then he should also be at the same level or perhaps slightly higher. If we have a particular social standing, then he should match that." Or they may say, "since our son has a degree, she should also have a degree, or at the least, a diploma." What is the need for all of this? What is there to prevent an educated woman who is a medical doctor from marrying a young religious man even if he never studied in high school? Who says they cannot come together in marriage or live happily? What law prevents this? Why are people always looking for a girl who looks a certain way or whose father has a particular social standing? There is no need for this. Islam does not accept these criteria because Islam insists on emphasizing spiritual values.

Islam encourages us to seek decency and chastity; incidentally, this is what actually brings about sweetness and joy to our lives. We mentioned the narration that if someone chooses a spouse because of her wealth or beauty, God can keep these qualities with her or take them away.[5] This is how reality operates. Many people become wealthy and then lose it all; many people are beautiful but their beauty fades. But the tradition also says that if you choose your spouse based on his or her religious devotion, you will be given wealth and

---

[5] Allah's Messenger: "Whoever marries a woman for her wealth, God will leave him to himself, and whoever marries a woman for her beauty, he will see in her that which repulses him, but whoever marries her due to her religion, God will gather for him all three." *Wasāʾil al-Shīʿah*, vol. 20, "Bāb istiḥbāb tazwīj al-marʾah li dīnihā ...".

beauty, and this is not because God will change the way they appear, but the way you feel about them. When you are filled with love and affection for someone, they become beautiful in your eyes. Beauty has more to do with your heart and your gaze than your partner's face.

Similarly, if a person is poor, God will provide for him wealth. But wealth does not mean that he will become financially rich; 'wealth' here means that he will be able to live his life in comfort and contentment and without difficulties. When young people are approached regarding marriage, they say, "but what will we do about an income and a home?" But these have always been the barriers that stand in the way of our fundamental life choices. God says in the Qurʾān:

$$\text{إِن يَكُونُوا فُقَرَاءَ يُغْنِهِمُ اللَّـهُ مِن فَضْلِهِ}$$

... If they are poor, Allah will enrich them out of His grace ... (Nūr, 24:32)

In other words, God will suffice them when they get married. Marriage will not bring about additional difficulty in their lives; on the contrary, God will enrich them with his grace. This is what God Himself says. Hence, we must pursue the values that Islam has emphasized for us.

There is a tradition in which Imam al-Sādiq (ʿa) tells someone who wants to get married, "Do you know you are looking for a lifetime partner? A person with whom you are going to spend your whole life. So pay attention to whom you choose! Check her morals, religiosity, and modesty before you go ahead with it." This is the type of spouse we need to choose. In another narration, it says that the most successful of men is one who is granted a wife by God, such that whenever he looks at her, he finds joy and happiness, and whenever he is absent from her, she protects his trust—the trust of his wealth, his secrets, and his dignity.

Those of you who have already chosen your spouse, you must now hold fast to your choice. Realize the worth of this bond and protect the institution of marriage.

Marriage in the Qurʾān

Regarding man and woman within the framework of marriage, the Qurʾān states:

وَمِنْ آيَاتِهِ أَنْ خَلَقَ لَكُم مِّنْ أَنفُسِكُمْ أَزْوَاجًا لِّتَسْكُنُوا إِلَيْهَا وَجَعَلَ بَيْنَكُم مَّوَدَّةً وَرَحْمَةً ۚ إِنَّ فِي ذَٰلِكَ لَآيَاتٍ لِّقَوْمٍ يَتَفَكَّرُونَ

"And of His signs is that He created for you spouses from among yourselves so that you may find rest in them, and He put between you love and compassion; most surely there are signs in this for a people who reflect."
(Rūm 30:21)[6]

Therefore, one of God's signs is that He made for you, spouses from your own kind—i.e., like you; for you men, he made women; and for you women, he made men. They are from you, "from your own selves." They are not from a different kind of species, nor do they belong to a different level, nor do they

---

[6]Ali Quli Qarai's translation of the Qurʾān has been utilized throughout this work and modified where necessary. [Ed.]

have different capacities; they are all from one origin, one source, and one reality. Of course, they are different in some respects but this is because of the different responsibilities assigned to them.

Next, the verse says, "that you may take comfort in them." The fact that the human species is composed of these two genders is not without reason: it is to provide peace and tranquillity. This means, for example, when you are by the side of your other half in your home—a man beside his wife and a woman beside her husband—you should feel at peace. A man feels relaxed when he comes home to a peaceful environment and has a kind, loving, and trustworthy wife by his side. And a woman feels happy and calm when she has a husband who is like a firm fortress—in so far as a man is physically stronger than a woman—for her to lean on and rely on, and who loves her dearly. The family environment is what provides this for both man and woman. A man can only find peace by having a wife, and a woman can only find peace by having a husband—"that you may take comfort in them." So both partners need each other to attain peace and tranquillity and mankind's most important need is peace. Mankind's happiness depends upon finding spiritual peace and being free from spiritual anxiety and conflict. This kind of peace can be provided to a man and a woman through married life.

The next part of the verse is quite beautiful. It says: "... and He ordained affection and mercy between you." This is the proper relation between man and woman: affection and kindness. It is to love each other and to be kind towards each other. Love with violence is not acceptable nor is kindness without love. The divinely inspired nature of man and woman within the context of the family is a nature that creates an inclusive relationship; this is the relationship of "affection and mercy." That which holds the family together is this very affection.

The Paragon of Marriage: ʿAlī and Fāṭimah

The best of all the daughters in the world and the best of all the sons in the world married each other with a customary dowry (*mahr al-sunnah*) that followed the example set by our Prophet (ṣ) and a very plain and simple marriage-gift. The life of Imam ʿAlī (ʿa) and Fāṭimah al-Zahrā (ʿa) should stand out as a model for us. The Commander of the Faithful, the best of all youth, married young and married the best woman to have ever lived. The worth of this man and the worth of this woman are incomparable to all the young men and women in the world. Moreover, Imam ʿAlī (ʿa) was not just the greatest youth from a spiritual point of view; he was also a heroic warrior on the battlefield. And Lady Fāṭimah (ʿa) was not just any daughter; she was the daughter of the most important man in the Islamic world of that time. Yet, a girl with such a position and a boy with such a status, married with a humble dowry and a humble marriage gift.

Do not surmise that just because this was a long time ago, there were no excessive dowries or marriage gifts, or that people at that time did not engage in this kind of behavior. In those days, much like today, when the daughter of an important tribal leader or a girl from a wealthy family was married, many elaborate gifts were prepared. For instance, some individuals would set the dowry for their daughters to be heavy gold coins, a hundred camels, a thousand dinars, or even ten thousand dinars. It was, in fact, one of the hallmarks of the Age of Ignorance (Jāhiliyyah), which the Prophet (ṣ) put an end to.

Both the Prophet (ṣ) and Imam ʿAlī (ʿa)—i.e., the families of the bride and groom—were considered nobles amongst the Quraysh; they were amongst the most honoured and magnanimous families of the Quraysh. Even though they were not bound to worldly matters, such as wealth and pride, they still enjoyed the highest status amongst the people of their time.

The groom in this wedding was the Commander of the Faithful (ʿa) who, even at this early stage of his life, had won great successes and made glorious accomplishments. The bride was none other than Fāṭimah al-Zahrā (ʿa), the daughter of the Prophet (ṣ), the most important man in Madinah; she was preeminent amongst all of the women in this nascent Muslim community. There should remain no doubt, that both the bride's family and the groom's family knew all about extravagance and dowries, but because they devalued worldly matters, they did not sully their spiritual union with such trivial things. Money, gold, and worldly wealth were far too insignificant to play any role in such a momentous occasion.

So what dowry did Fāṭimah al-Zahrā (ʿa) receive? What was her marriage gift? How was her wedding? Her dowry consisted of those few things recorded in the books of history: a reed mat, a brush made of palm fibres, a set of bedding, a quern, a jug, and a bowl.[7] If you want to know the value of

---

[7] *Biḥār al-anwār*, vol. 43, "Kitāb tarīkh Fāṭimah wa Ḥasan wa Ḥusayn, Abwāb tārīkh Sayyidah al-Nisā' al-ʿālamīn, Bāb tazwijihā," ḥadīth no. 5.

her dowry in today's currency, it would be just under twenty dollars! Of everything she was given as a marriage gift, there was nothing worth even so much as a normal item of clothing today. Now this is something to emulate. It was not that the Prophet (ṣ) could not provide more for his daughter; had he wished, there were plenty of companions who would have happily brought any amount of money or furnishings as a gift to the bride and groom; but the Prophet (ṣ) did not want this. The Prophet (ṣ) chose a simple marriage gift and a humble dowry for a reason; he wanted others to learn from it. We know now that in the Prophet's (ṣ) household, all the young men and women did not marry with a dowry higher than the one established by the Prophet (ṣ) (*mahr al-sunnah*). They did not ensnare themselves with appearances.

We do not have the capacity to do what they did, but they have made the path clear for us. They have given us the key for embarking on our married lives together. There is no way we can compare our lives to theirs; we do not expect anyone, not even ourselves, to match the Prophet's (ṣ) Household in this regard. Nonetheless, they represent the pinnacle and we must strive as best as we can to walk towards it, seeking closeness to it.

Let us not turn our gaze to those who represent the satanic pinnacle on the opposite side and who hold extravagant weddings. They existed in the Islamic era as they exist today. When Maʾmūn, the Abbasid Caliph, got married, he showered his wife with boxes of gold. This was in addition to the jewels, gold, and sweets that were distributed during the wedding ceremony. When the guests opened up these boxes, they found deeds for the ownership of property and lands. Of course, these lands and properties were usurped from others in the first place and were now freely being given away. When wealth is gained through illicit means, it is spent extravagantly. In fact, they had gone to such excesses that even Ma'mūn agreed it was a waste. It was precisely these excesses that would cause Islam to suffer defeat for many centuries after him and become the victim of the onslaught of many nations.

An Islamic Occasion

Our advice to the brides and grooms and to their families is to try to make the marriage ceremony an Islamic one. To 'Islamicize' the marriage ceremony does not imply that there is no celebration, joviality, merrymaking, or the opportunity to host guests; on the contrary, an Islamic marriage, like other marriages, contains elements of celebration, joviality, and enjoying guests. In fact, having a feast (walīmah) for the marriage and inviting others as guests is recommended (mustaḥab) in Islam. When we say that the marriage ceremony should be 'Islamic' we do not intend to remove these elements; rather, what we mean to say is that prior to the wedding ceremony, during it, and after it, nothing should be done that is against Islam. Now, as soon as we say "against Islam", one automatically thinks of inappropriate gender interaction, forbidden types of music, etc. Of course, these are "against Islam" but so are many other things. For example, extravagance is against Islam. Hence, when we are excessive in our food and drink, when we are excessive in spending, and when we are excessive in ornamentation—i.e., whenever we go beyond the acceptable limits—these are all forms of extravagance and are religiously forbidden. Unfortunately, this definitively forbidden tendency is widespread amongst the people to one extent or another. They turn this occasion of marriage—something that could actually bring about God's favour on them—into a sin through their extravagances, their violations, and their merging of this noble act with the forbidden deeds that they perform. Inappropriate gender interaction is not the only thing forbidden in Islam; excessive spending is also forbidden; extravagance is also forbidden; making the have-nots feel bad is definitely forbidden in some cases; using illicit income in order to prepare the marriage gift is also forbidden.

Some people spend a fortune on a wedding dress. What is the need for this? If it is worn for one night, you can rent a dress as some people do. There is nothing wrong with this. It is not shameful in the least, despite what others may think. What is truly shameful is when a person pays an exorbitant amount of money for something that they only wear once and has no need for after. A one-time use! This is especially shameful when we are aware of the situation of some people who are truly destitute.

If marriage ceremonies are held in a way such that a large portion of the population feel they cannot live up to that standard, then daughters will remain in their parents' homes and sons will remain unmarried. This is a sin and we should see it as that. Sometimes, we are so focused on the minute sins that we forget about the greater ones.

This anti-Islamic practice is often spread by those individuals who do not need to worry about their finances. They rent expensive and extravagant halls to hold such ceremonies and to invite guests; they buy noticeably expensive clothes and perform unnecessary things that no one has done before in order to outdo others. There are times when something is innovative and original, which adds beauty without being costly, and there is nothing wrong with this. However, there are times when large sums of money are spent for such things, and this is wasteful; it is ostentation and can be very dangerous. It is precisely because of such ostentatious displays that many of our young men and women are deprived of marriage. All of these heavy dowries, expensive marriage gifts, and extravagant get-togethers have caused young men and women to remain without a partner. When Islam instructs us to do something, there is always a wisdom behind it. Islamic law and all of the divine teachings spring from divine wisdom. I honestly believe those who make life difficult for others—by holding such extravagant weddings, setting high dowries, and preparing expensive marriage gifts—will face a severe accounting with God.

The problem with extravagance does not only arise for those who spend without having the means; it is a problem even if you have the means but spend it wastefully. In fact, it is normally those who have money who are the most wasteful. This is one problem. The other problem is that it fosters a sense of competition and jealousy in other individuals. Consequently, those who cannot attain the same standard, whether it be the bride, the groom, or their families, will feel deficient. There are so many young men and women, who even after marriage, feel inadequate and dissatisfied, develop an inferiority complex, and become bitter all because of the wasteful spending of the wealthy. Countless marriages are delayed for this reason and young men and women remain unmarried. These are the two essential problems with extravagance, although if you dig deeper, you will likely find many more auxiliary problems. When you are extravagant, you are harming not only yourself but others as well—the young men and women that are affected by your excess. You are bringing yourself down in the eyes of the Prophet (ṣ) and the Imam of the Age (ʿa). Therefore, I strongly advise you to make your marriage ceremonies as simple as possible.

These extravagant functions in big hotels with lots of expenses were what the supporters of the Shah's regime used to do, whereas we used to host our weddings in our homes in one or two rooms. If we did not have space, we would ask the neighbours to help us. We would put out some sweets and fruits; we sat, talked, laughed, joked, and had lots of fun. In comparison, the Shah and his people—whose presence we no longer need to tolerate thank God—were not satisfied with simple weddings; they organized large, expensive, and elaborate functions in hotels. Now that we have replaced their regime, we must not follow in their footsteps. If we do, we will become just like them. Some may surmise that we should avoid this only if we cannot afford it; but once we have the means, there is nothing wrong in having such grand functions. This is not what true logic dictates.

Marriages and festivities are good in and of themselves. Even the Prophet himself (ṣ) had a wedding celebration for his beloved daughter where people rejoiced and recited poetry and the women clapped; it was a happy occasion. Therefore, having a wedding celebration, rejoicing, offering food, and being happy are all good things; there is no problem with it. If anyone tells me that wedding festivities are occurring in any corner of our country and a group of people are happy and rejoicing, I will be happy too. But extravagance, excessiveness, and ostentation are wrong; we must be careful that they do not creep into our festivity. Inviting guests for a wedding feast is good, but it should be short, simple, modest, and honourable. Set up a simple get-together, warm and cordial, and invite some family and friends—a few friends of the bride, a few friends of the groom, and a few friends of the parents. Then share some sweets together, make conversation, and spend half a day in merriment. At the end, you may return to your homes while the newlyweds go to theirs. This is how it should be. But extravagance and waste is not good; in fact, sometimes more food is thrown out at weddings than is actually eaten! We must put a stop to this. For those couples getting married, be careful to avoid this because there is no need for it. All of the pressure on the families of the bride and groom are unnecessary.

Strengthening the Marital Bond

Marriage is a divine blessing, and every blessing deserves gratitude. The gratitude owed for this blessing is to strive in safeguarding the marriage bond and not to let trivial affairs, grievances, pointless accusations, excessive argumentation, and cutting exorbitant expenditures disrupt it and threaten the integrity of the family—a family that was formed through the marriage contract. By reciting the formula of this contract, which is a conventional matter, a certain bond forms between the couple. As such, the husband and wife must exert their utmost effort in preserving this bond.

At this stage of life, which is the most important and significant of any person's life, everyone wants the marriage to begin with health and happiness. But it is up to the two of you, the couple, to make sure that it begins this way and stays this way. A couple must abide by the following criteria: anything that weakens the foundation of marriage should be abstained from. For instance, unnecessary complaints, high expectations, or excessive strictness would spoil the intimacy and cut off relations in a family. You cannot gain intimacy in your marriage life with money, power, or anything else. So do not let this sacred relationship be ruined by complaints and misery, greed and expectations, lack of affection and emotional distance, or the interference of others in your married life. The point of utmost importance here is that both parties of the marriage try their best to protect this marital bond.

How can you protect this bond? Of course, people who are wise and sensitive realize that they must protect it through mutual trust and affection; they must neither force their opinions on the other nor expect too much from them. They must be each other's closest friend and companion if they are to protect the family structure. If both parties do what is expected of them, then this marriage will not only be blessed, but by God's will it will increase in blessings. Its fate lies in our hands.

One kind of blessing in marriage takes shape when both the man and the woman feel that they have certain responsibilities and obligations towards one another that must be observed. Begin this new stage of your life with this in mind; in marriage, each one of the couple completes the other and neither is whole without the other. You must never assume that one partner is more important than the other in order for the marriage to work. For example, some people say that the man is more important and dominant whereas the woman is subordinate, or vice versa. We do not agree with this. Neither partner is dominant nor subordinate; rather, the combination of the two, side-by-side, is what matters. Both partners need each other, not only sexually but also emotionally, spiritually, and religiously. A woman gives comfort to a man and a man brings security to a woman. Neither person should think they are better than the other. Each couple is like the two hinges of a door; without one, the other would be ineffective. A couple is like a compound word, meaning that if you take away one part of it, the other part makes no sense. This is what being a couple means and you must enter married life with this perspective in mind.

Being Grateful for Marriage

Protect and appreciate this bond, and know that it is a divine blessing. Everything that you have is from God:

$$\text{وَمَا بِكُم مِّن نِّعْمَةٍ فَمِنَ اللَّـهِ ۖ ثُمَّ إِذَا مَسَّكُمُ الضُّرُّ فَإِلَيْهِ تَجْأَرُونَ}$$

Whatever blessing you have is from Allah, and when a distress befalls you, you make entreaties to Him. (16:53)

It is very important to pay attention to this blessing just as you would for other blessings. Sometimes, individuals do not appreciate the blessings they have, just as others do not appreciate the importance of what is happening when they get married. It is as if they have attended someone else's social gathering; there is some momentary frivolity and joy, but that is all! It should not be this way. Marriage comes with vows and commitments; but with these commitments, come blessings that make them ever so sweet. Some people get married, are blessed with a good spouse, and have a lovely life, but fail to see what a huge blessing this is. When they do not see this, they forget to be thankful to God and therefore deprive themselves of the divine mercy that comes along with being thankful. People need to recognize how blessed they are.

Now how can we be grateful for such a blessing? Sometimes we only give thanks verbally while our hearts do not share the sentiment! This kind of gratitude is done merely out of habit and has no value whatsoever. In cases such as these, our words go no further than our lips and they will definitely not find a way to the Divine Throne. But there are also times when we truly appreciate the blessing and are thankful to God from the bottom of our hearts. To recognize that God has blessed us and to be truly grateful for it is indeed precious. However, when we are giving thanks to God, we also need to somehow demonstrate this gratitude. Now that God has granted us this blessing, what can we do?

God does not expect much from us in return for the blessings He has granted us; He does not ask us to go and perform some difficult task as compensation. The only real expectation God has of us in return for His blessings is that we look after them. This is not asking for too much. Since God has endowed us with this blessing, He simply wants us to treat it well. In Islam, this just means abiding by family ethics and principles. How should we live our life so that it is a good life? Much has been said about this in many books and in different languages, but here I would like to present a portion of it.

THE FAMILY, THE WORLD'S FIRST INSTITUTION

The Role of the Family in Society

My first piece of advice is that you give importance to the idea of forming a family. One must emphasize the role and position of the home; it is unthinkable that a person should have no home or place of comfort. Every person needs a home and a homely environment, and the soul of this environment is the family. We must give this issue importance and reflect over it. There are conditions, obligations, and etiquettes at this stage, and this brings about both rights and responsibilities. The most prominent aspect of this is the formation of a new social order. Although marriage brings about many benefits for men and women alike—birth of children, fulfilling desires, etc.—the pivot around which all of these revolve is the family bond. This is the core principle.

Therefore, all of your efforts must go into protecting this bond, for it is like adding a new cell into the ever-changing cells of a societal body. Your cells are always changing, and you need a constant influx of new cells so that your body lives and grows. By forming a family, you are adding a new cell to the body of society; so try your best to make sure that this cell is healthy, happy, energetic, and a source of pride and success for its society. Each family is a cell in a societal body. When that cell is healthy and prosperous, the body of society is healthy. This does not mean that if a cell is healthy or unhealthy, it will affect the other cells; however, it does mean that if the individual cells are healthy, then the body as a whole will also be healthy. The body is comprised of cells. Every organ is a collection of cells. So if we can keep the cells healthy, we have guaranteed the health of that organ. This is how important marriage is.

If you want marriage to be this way, then you must follow the religious etiquettes and limits that have been prescribed for the family; anything that helps to protect the new family bond is good and pleases God. On the other hand, if, God forbid, something shakes the foundation of this bond, then that thing is something harmful and should be avoided. Marriage is not like the other events in a person's life; rather, it is a whole new stage of living and a crossroads. Some people who have set out on this journey and find themselves at a crossroads are not able to make it through on the "straight path" due to their own situation, that of their spouse, or the general conditions of their family. However, others are able to make it through. If you wish to traverse through the "straight path", you should follow the religious guidelines and give importance to the family ethics that the divine religion has mandated. The very first of these is to appreciate the value of this new bond.

The family is a source of tranquillity for a human being, and no one can truly enjoy the sweetness of life without a tranquil family environment. Each family is a centre for the growth and nourishment of several souls. If you break up the family unit and have the children raised by friends and associates, as opposed to being raised within the family unit, they will not grow well. If you take them and place them in an institution or a day care like an incubator for chicks, where a [foreign] person is tasked with nurturing them, they will not be raised as human beings. This is simply the nature of a human being. God created human beings in a way that is very different from other creatures. There are some species of animals in which the newborn never sees its parents; some parents die after releasing their eggs and this is their nature. And whether these animals meet their parents or not, they will still grow up to be just like them. But humans are not like this.

God created man as a learner; he must learn many things. Moreover, if he is brought up in the company of his parents—with their love, their friendship, and their attention—then he will not be devoid of anything from a spiritual point of view. However, if from a young age, he is taken from his small [personal] environment and placed in a large [impersonal] one, he will not blossom as this flower is meant to blossom. This is the particularity of man and it is why God has placed affection into the hearts of parents for their children, because it is precisely this affection that will nourish that child. Such affection is part of human nature; this is why it exists and why every child has an affectionate relationship with his parents. The love and affection that you have for your children is the same love and affection that your parents had for you; it is also the same affection that your child will have for his or her children in turn. This affection comes from marriage, which is the foundation of the family environment.

A family is a "good word" (kalimah tayyibah)[8]; the particularity of a "good word" is that wherever it appears, it becomes a constant source of goodness and blessings, influencing everything around it. A "good word" includes any God-given gift that is based on a true foundation. Each family is a micro-society; initially, it is made up of a man and a woman and gradually expands with the arrival of children, then grandchildren, just as a tree grows and gains new branches and leaves and then bears fruit. God loves such micro-societies.

It is impossible for an Islamic society to progress—especially in terms of its culture—without the foundation of healthy, happy, and energetic families. Therefore having a family is essential. Now some may object to our words by saying that the West seem to be progressing despite the loss of the family structure. However, the effects of the ever-more prevalent destruction of family life in the West cannot be seen immediately but will eventually become apparent. Global and historical changes do not reveal their effects

---

[8] Referring to verse 24 of Surah Ibrāhīm: "Have you not regarded how Allah has drawn a parable? A good word is like a good tree: its roots are steady and its branches are in the sky." (14:24)

right away; rather, they do so over time. But the effects have already begun to take shape.

When the West reached the height of its advancement, it still had strong family values. Even in matters of sexuality there were some ethical codes—albeit different from the Islamic codes but valid in their own right—that they abided by. Any individual familiar with Western history is aware of this fact both in Europe and later in America. There were codes for social interaction between the two sexes; the concept of modesty and preventing situations that could lead to accusations of indecency existed as well. However, unconstrained libertinism has gradually become the norm in the West; its seeds were sown then and the result is what we see today. The present situation, likewise, will result in a hard and bitter tomorrow for that society.

Why does the West expend so much effort to promote hedonism in Eastern countries in general and Muslim countries in particular? One reason is to shatter the family unit and weaken their cultures in order to dominate them. Until and unless the culture of a nation is weakened, it is not possible to bridle it, to put reins on it, to mount it, and then to steer it. Losing one's cultural identity leaves a nation defenceless and at the mercy of foreign invaders. It becomes easy for enemies and imperialists to do this when the foundation of the family in a society is undermined.

When the family unit is shaken, social ethics are affected; the solid, age-old practices that bring felicity to a nation and that are the result of centuries of collective experiences, quickly vanish. As you know, each society develops a particular series of values based on the wise contemplations of its forerunners and sages—if they are divine—and these become the basis of that society. These codes of conduct—such as being faithful to one another or being trustworthy— are upheld by the people, irrespective of whether or not they are written down. However, when the family unit is destroyed, these traditional values cannot be passed on from one generation to the next. Children cannot inherit any of these values from their parents. Faith is not passed down; and neither are spiritual virtues and attributes. This is a major loss for any society and is the direct result of the break-up of the family.

A society devoid of the family is an agitated society, a restless society. It is a society in which the cultural and intellectual heritage cannot easily be transferred from one generation to the next. When a society lacks strong families to form its foundation, even its best centres for bringing up children cannot nourish them.

A good family, then, is one in which both partners are kind, faithful, and intimate with one another; they show one another love and affection; they look out for one another; and they respect and give importance to each other's best interests. This is the first step.

Next, they feel a sense of responsibility towards the children that are born into their family; they help them maintain their physical and spiritual wellbeing; they educate them, encourage them to engage in certain things and keep away from other things, and imbue virtuous qualities within them. Such a family becomes the source of all true reforms in a country. This is because individuals in such a family are nurtured well and are raised with good qualities such as bravery, intelligence, thoughtfulness, responsibility, kindness, confidence, decisiveness, altruism, and nobility. Now, if a society is composed of people with such excellent qualities—i.e., if they are altruistic, noble, brave, intelligent, thoughtful, and effective—that society would seldom face a calamity. A society composed of such families will be reformed and protected. If a reformer rises up in the community, he would be able to reform that society through the existing families; but if there were no [stable] families, even the greatest reformer would not be able to reform such a society.

The Family Institution

Islam wishes that such an institution be created. The genius of Islam, as with all genuine religions, is that it directs man's sexual desire and the desire for companionship (the two being distinct in so far as the latter is more general than the former) towards making a family. These religions have set up the institution of the family and ensured its preservation in such a way that it is supported by man's desires. At a certain age, some people may lose their sexual appetite, but the desire for companionship with the opposite gender remains strong. This applies to both men and women. A home is the source of one's tranquillity. This is why Islam and all religions have made these natural desires the foundation for forming a family.

Now, if people were free to satisfy their natural desires in whatever manner they pleased, it would lead to one of two consequences: either it would be fulfilled without the blessing of a family, or if a family was formed, it would be a weak, vulnerable, and empty one—a unit that would collapse with the slightest breeze. This is why wherever you see a nation that promotes complete sexual freedom, the family unit is weak, because men and women in that country do not need the institution of the family to fulfil their desires. In contrast, when you see a nation that is governed by religion and where libertinism does not exist, a man and a woman will find everything they need [through marriage] and, hence, this institution will be preserved.

If men and women engage in sexual activities outside of the house—in their social gatherings, at work, at school, or at other inappropriate venues—the greatest harm that can come about is that the strong bond between a man and a woman and their family as a whole will be torn to shreds. A man or woman who satisfies his or her sexual desire outside the context of the family will not find the prospect of forming a family as attractive as would a chaste couple—i.e., a man who knows no other woman as he knows his wife, and a woman who knows no other man as she knows her husband.

Wherever hedonism or libertinism takes root and ethical ruptures appear, the rupture of the family follows suit. The result of this can be clearly seen in the Western world of today, especially in countries where permissiveness is more widespread. In these places, the term 'family' does not carry its normal connotation. If our media would report more news from the West about its growing family crisis and the real situation of men, women, and children living there, our own people would realize that the strong fabric of the family in our society is in fact a tremendous blessing.

Family: an Abode of Peace

The Qur'ān describes the relationship between a man and a woman with the word *sakan*, which means a source of rest and tranquillity. When we say 'rest', we do not wish to contrast it with a state of motion (since motion is something good); rather, we wish to contrast it to a state of agitation. Sometimes man is stricken with agitation in life and it is this *sakan* which gives him the repose he needs so that he does not become distraught in that situation.

There are a few verses of the Qur'ān that we need to pay attention to in this regard. The first is from Surah al-Rūm:

$$وَمِن آياتِهِ أَن خَلَقَ لَكُم مِن أَنفُسِكُم أَزواجًا لِتَسكُنوا إِلَيها$$

And of His signs is that He created for you spouses from among yourselves so that you may find rest in them ...
(Rūm, 30:21)

In other words, one of the signs of God's divine power is that he created the human race—i.e., men and women—in pairs so that this can be a source of tranquillity for them. This is not exclusive to men such that one supposes that God created women for the tranquillity of men; rather, it is a mutual benefit—i.e., God created men for the tranquillity of women as well. This is what forms the family atmosphere. The inner precincts of the family are permeated with a spirit of peace for both the man and woman who live within it.

Another verse is from Surah al-Naḥl, in which God says:

$$ وَاللَّـهُ جَعَلَ لَكُم مِن بُيُوتِكُم سَكَنًا $$

It is Allah who has made your homes as a place of rest
(sakan) for you ... (Naḥl, 16:80)

These homes that God has made into a place of rest ostensibly refers to the family habitat.

In Surah Aʿrāf, God says:

$$ وَجَعَلَ مِنها زَوجَها لِيَسكُنَ إِلَيها $$

... and made from it its mate, that he might find comfort
(yaskuna) with her ... (Aʿrāf, 7:189)

God gave us spouses from ourselves so that we can find repose and peace by their side. The kind of peace that a husband finds with his wife, or at home, or in a safe and serene family environment is one that he cannot find anywhere else.

Life is a struggle. In fact, the entirety of a human being's lifespan is one long struggle. It can take on different forms: struggle with nature, struggle with various obstacles in society, and struggle with one's own inner soul. Man is forever struggling. Even the human body is constantly locked in a battle with potentially harmful organisms and elements; when it has enough strength to fight them, it remains healthy. This struggle in every man must be proper, orderly, in the right direction, and undertaken with the right tools. It must also have a base and an asylum. This struggle is like a journey and the way station or resting stop is the family habitat. A man must feel this repose when he is with his family.

Whether you are a man or a woman, you will face battles and struggles in society, at work, and at school since life is full of struggles. Even if a woman is a housewife and not working outside, she will still face struggles in her life and in her interactions with other people. In all aspects of life, the human being must struggle—there are things he desires but cannot obtain. We are forever struggling to overcome obstacles, and as these obstacles wear us down and sap our strength, we need a haven in which to recuperate, and this haven is nothing other than the family. The family environment is a person's haven of tranquillity and centre of peace.

Men and women, each in their own way, have struggles in their daily tasks, in education, in employment, and in social, political, and humanitarian activities for the sake of God. They each need a shelter in this big society, not only to rest their weary bodies, but also their minds and souls—and that shelter is the family.

It is in this context, that the role of a woman becomes clear, because only she can create a family environment filled with love, gentleness, and affection. It is like a pool of fresh, clean water. When an exhausted person smeared with dirt enters a pool of water, it rejuvenates him, invigorates him, and washes away the grime from his body. The family sanctuary is no different—when an individual tainted with the dirt and grime of social activities enters his home, it cools him down, refreshes him, and grants him repose. Only a woman can provide this when she puts her heart into her home.

The family and its warm environment is the place where a man's inner agitations can be pacified. A family is a small assemblage—it begins with two and gradually grows with God's blessings; even if it multiplies into a family of ten or fifteen, its subsistence is still dependent on those two initial members. This small assemblage is like an ocean. You have seen how a river flows—it flows wildly, raving from side to side, colliding with and eroding its banks ... until it reaches the ocean. The ocean is where the river water comes to a rest. All that fervour and agitation is transformed into peace in the ocean. This is what the home can do.

Every individual, regardless of gender, experiences distress due to unforeseen incidents, unexpected difficulties, and long tiring hours at work. This distress—whether it is psychological, emotional, mental, or physical—can lead to agitation and restlessness within a person. Hence, when a man enters his house, the family environment should be a sanctuary of peace; this is how God has envisioned the family. The same is true for women, regardless of whether she works outside the house or within the house. In fact, contrary to what some people assume, working at home can be more difficult than working outside—it can be physically and mentally more taxing since she is managing the household. Like everything else, it has its challenges and these challenges can bring about stress. Women must put up with the difficulties of life—jealousy, inconsideration, belittlement, and backbiting—not to mention the difficulties of doing the housework and caring for the children. All of these are sources of distress for a woman who stays at home; so when her husband comes home it is as if her godsent reliever has come to rescue her. The family habitat now becomes a garden for both of them. Is this a negative thing? It is the most basic necessity for any human being and every couple should strive to achieve this. Of course, this will not magically spring into being; it requires preparation and effort. But it is not impossible. When both the husband and the wife utilize their intellects, they will succeed.

All men and women must strive to foster this peaceful family environment; neither of them should be the cause of disturbing this peace. An immoral man, an ill-tempered woman, an over-critical man, a demanding woman ... these are the types of people who can ruin the tranquillity of the family habitat and prevent the actualization of the verse "that you may take comfort in them." Islam has the power to intelligently transform the lives of individuals into a kind of heaven on Earth as long as its teachings are followed properly; but if the husband and wife disrupt this abode of peace by overstepping the bounds, engaging in unnecessary argumentation, and being inappropriately critical of each other, there will be no peace remaining.

The Qur'ān foresees the possibility of peace and repose for the husband and wife when it says, "you may take comfort in them." But what does 'repose' mean? Repose is when a person finds a moment of relief, a safe harbour from all the stresses of life that are inevitable in this world. A husband and wife that stand right beside each other and are truly a pair (zawj) will seek refuge in each other during these times of distress—the woman will turn to her husband and the man will turn to his wife.

A husband caught up in the tussles of a man's world is in need of a moment of peace in order to recuperate and continue with his obligations. When is that moment of peace? It is when he enters the precincts of his family—a place brimming with love and affection. When the man encounters his wife and feels united with her, that is his moment of peace and comfort. It is the same for a woman. In the tussles of a woman's world—regardless of whether she is working at home, in the public sphere, or involved in various political or social activities—she encounters many challenges and difficulties.

Recognizing the Value of Domestic Work

A woman's responsibility in the house is in no way less important or less taxing than her public responsibilities; if anything, it is quite the opposite. Managing the house is a vocation—a great vocation, an important vocation, a precarious vocation, and a vocation that will build the future. Having children is a difficult undertaking and raising them is not an easy task. Consider any type of work that seems strenuous; compare it to raising children and you will find it easy. Raising children is truly an art. A man would have extreme difficulty doing it for even a day, yet a woman bears this task with great precision, determination, and finesse every day. God has truly endowed her with tremendous ability in this regard. Nevertheless, raising children is undoubtedly a struggle that can wear out a person and bring them to their knees.

A woman plays a pivotal role in the family; but this does not absolve the man from having duties or responsibilities within his family or downplay his role within it. A man who is unconcerned with his family, who has no real attachment to it, who is engrossed in amusement, and who does not appreciate the hard work of his wife is undermining the family ambience. A man must recognize the value of a woman in her house. Society must recognize this value. It is imperative that we give particular importance to the work that a woman does inside her house. There are some women who had the opportunity to get a job but chose not to; there are some women who had the opportunity to pursue higher education, but opted against it; there are some women who already possessed degrees in higher education—and I know examples of these women—but they all decided to focus on their children and provide them a good upbringing instead of pursuing a career. The career they gave up was not left vacant for it was filled by other candidates; but those women decided to focus on something else. It is the value of this type of woman that we need to appreciate.

As the managers of the family, women have to put in a lot of hard work and energy to run the household as a unit. A homemaker is someone who has full control over the running of the household and the family environment. It is a tedious and delicate job, and only a woman's finesse can meet the challenge. No man can take account of all the intricacies involved nor even begin to understand them. However, God has created this finesse within the nature of women.

Consider the following analogy: If one wants to dig out rocks from the ground, a person with large hefty fingers would be suited for this job. If this same person is now asked to handle or pick up tiny gems, he may not be able to. Similarly, a person with fine delicate hands may not be able to dig out a large rock, but he would be able to gather tiny gems from the ground. Men and women are like this; each have responsibilities and it is not possible to say one partner's responsibility is harder than the other; both are difficult and both are necessary. When a woman becomes stressed from the tussles of life, in so far as her soul is delicate, she is in need of relief and comfort, not to mention a stronghold that she can rely on. That stronghold is her husband. This is how God has put the two together. If they are able to keep the family ambience healthy, these two will remain together.

Some people wrongly suppose that if we equate a woman's primary work to that which takes place within the household, this is demeaning for women. This is not demeaning at all; on the contrary, the most important work for a woman is to keep life going for the family. There are two fundamental elements in a family: the man and the woman; the former is the worker while the latter is the caretaker. If the woman wishes to become a worker and seek an income, there is nothing in Islam preventing her from doing this; however, this is not her responsibility nor is it something that is required of her. That which is required of her is to protect the living ambience of the collective family; initially, this collectivity includes only the husband and wife, but later it proceeds to include all the children as well.

One of most crucial needs of a human being is a calm family environment. When a man and a woman come together to make a family, they must show kindness and affection to one another; this mutual love and affection fills them both with peace and gives them the energy to continue with their lives. When the wife feels that her husband is beside her and she can rely on him, and when the husband feels that his wife is on his side and loves him, then all the agitations of life are subsumed in an aura of peace. This is the meaning of the Qur'ānic term *sakan*.

If the husband and wife are both compassionate and act according to what is right, then this state of *sakan* will begin at the onset of marriage and continue, God-willing, until they are an elderly couple. Of course, there may be differences in tastes or preferences, but these are not important and will not disrupt the state of peace in the family.

A woman should know that sometimes her presence can touch a man's soul more so than anything else can. She can bring warmth to a man's heart, grant him hope in life, and encourage him to continue his efforts. She has the capacity to even infuse a man with strength and that is how important her role is. A man also has a similar effect on a woman. Now, there may be a time when a man comes home in an irritable mood. In this situation, a wise and experienced woman will not react to his irritability. If she can do this, and respond to him with love and a smile, gradually she will be able to open up the knots of his irascibility and incivility through the charm of her love and see what he truly needs.

Natural Human Desires

When we speak of creating tranquillity within the family, there is an element that is often ignored, and that is the natural sexual desire that everyone has for the opposite gender. Islam directs this instinctual desire to support the formation of the family. In other words, it states that an individual is not permitted to use this resource of the sexual drive anywhere other than within the family; its domain lies within the family. It is true that this desire is a human need and it should be fulfilled, but when it is used to support the foundation of a family, it now becomes a solid factor in preserving the longevity of the family. It is imperative to realize that if a husband or wife, God-forbid, uses this resource elsewhere, it will weaken the family foundation to the extent that it is utilized outside its precincts. On the surface, the face of the family may remain the same, but the basic building material of the family—i.e., the love, affection, attachment, and attraction between the man and the woman—will subside. This will bring about the same malady that is unfortunately being witnessed in most western families, particularly in America and Northern Europe.

A man and a woman may appear to be in the same family; their names are both written on the same marriage document. Religiously they have said the words and performed the marriage rituals, but the essential binding material between them is missing. This is because they have spent the valuable reserves of their natural desires elsewhere; what was meant to be the fuel of the family has been used in other places. In fact, they do not even feel the need for each other. They may address each other with titles such as "my dear", but these are mere words on the tongue. This is the same kind of "my dear" they could use to announce a divorce: "my dear, I would like to file for divorce." It means nothing. The word that we use in Persian, *azīzam*, which carries all the meanings of honour and respect does not exist in the English "my dear" which has become a norm nowadays.

Occasionally, such couples have school-aged children at primary and secondary levels who barely get to see the family together. Their lifestyle is not like ours whereby we get the opportunity to sit around the *sufrah* or dining table together—one passes the bread, the other asks for some food on his plate, while another asks "what about my food?" This is a sweet and amusing experience. The common table talk that occurs—"Why did the food turn out like this?", "How come you didn't make that today," "Could we have pasta for dinner?"—are words that those without a close-knit family never have the joy of hearing. Instead, the lady of the house gets a sandwich from her workplace or goes out to a coffee shop to grab something to eat with a colleague; the man has his own plans; and the children wander about aimlessly, and purchase whatever ready-made snacks they can find to fill their stomachs. Then they go loitering around inside their school and outside their school until they return home. If they do not find their parents at home, they go out again or spend their time watching television.

Since even these families realize that their situation is less than ideal, and in order to give a kind of routine to their lives, they set aside special times for the family to be together. But this is a contrived and artificial family ambience. It is an environment in which the man is constantly checking his watch so as not to be late for his night out with his friends or to go watch a movie; the woman has her own plans, and the children have made arrangements with their friends. They are all waiting anxiously for this family time to end. This is the extent of the disorder the family unit has reached in some places.

Now, there are some newspapers that keep ranting about the rate of divorce in our country. Let us assume that divorce has increased significantly, which could be the result of many foolish mistakes; however, it is not because of the dangerous lifestyle that dominates in the West. With the grace of God, we still have the binding material of love within our families. As long as this basis of sexual desire—which makes the man and woman dependent on each other—remains within the family, the individual will have protected half of his faith [through marriage] as the ḥadīth tells us. This is because man's lust can rob him of half of his faith. It is a tragic truth that man's innate sexual desire can steal half of his faith at any moment of his life from youth to old age. Hence, if you can contain this sexual desire, this influential devil, in a container and cap it, and let a part of it out when you need to and only within the marriage, then it will take you to a proper family structure. Those who are attentive will realize why Islam has taken a certain stance when it comes to gender interaction between a *maḥram* and a *non-maḥram*—for example, why is it that a woman should not adorn herself before going out; why should she not converse with a man flauntingly; why should a man not gaze at a woman with lust? The reason for all these regulations is to strengthen the foundation of the small family unit. In this way, the heart and eyes of a woman will not be deflected elsewhere nor will the heart and eyes of a man wander elsewhere. What will result is a strong family unit.

Positive Upbringing of Children

Another important issue to consider is children. The first place in which a person's soul, emotions, and thoughts can be kindled is within the family. In fact, it begins before the person is born and is influenced by a number of different factors. There are, undoubtedly, external forces as well—a person's school, neighbourhood, friends, teachers, books, etc.—which can influence children in their youth and adolescence. All of these can certainly change a child's way of thinking and can sometimes override the influence of the family. Nevertheless, what ultimately sets the stage is the family ambience. It is within the family that a child can be nurtured to be decent, inquisitive, helpful, affectionate, and considerate, or they could be raised to be the opposite. A couple's relationship with each other—whether it be healthy or detrimental—can have a tremendous effect on the family ambience. Hence, the tie that binds the marriage and family can leave an important, lasting, and fateful impact not only on the family itself but also on society as a whole. This is not a minor issue; it is of great importance. Therefore, let us take this matter seriously, and exert all that we have to make the family atmosphere a healthy one, coupled with mutual love and trust.

Having children is one of a woman's most important responsibilities, as well as one of her greatest challenges. Bringing up children is truly an art for women; it is she who must bear the difficulties and it is to her that God has granted the means of upbringing. He did not give this ability to men, but to women. He granted her patience; He gifted her with affection; He endowed her with sensitivity; and He invested her with a body to bear it. This is a woman's talent.

Hence, I advise all families, and especially the mothers, to pay close attention to children's hygiene and diet, as the best food for an infant is breast milk. It was very popular under the previous regime to follow the Western fad of feeding your baby formula and mothers were doing everything they could to avoid breast-feeding. Islam does not approve of this. Fortunately, these days, scientists have confirmed that breastfeeding is best and encourage mothers to practice this; breast milk is the best milk for a child. It is important to provide healthy, pure, and good food for your children. Families need to increase in size. The custom of limiting the number of children, as is common today, is not right.

The Binding Matter of Love

Another issue I want to raise is that in a family, both the husband and wife need to feel responsible towards one another. They should not think that they are two individuals who have simply decided to live together under the same roof. They are actually two parts of a single reality, two sides of the same coin. They are a *zawj*, which means a pair. If one of them is taken out of the equation, the other is incomplete; in other words, each one of them completes the other.

Allow me to offer an analogy. A couple is like two comrades defending a single bunker; their fates are inextricably bound together. When one of them sleeps, the other stands guard and vice versa. Neither of them can escape their collective fate, a fate that can be undermined by either one of them or both. They are connected together, and if they wish to survive, they must keep this connection in mind. The more they are able to strengthen this partnership, the more beneficial it will be for them. If you ask me how they can strengthen this bond, it is through love and affection.

When the marriage formula is recited, love finds its way into the hearts of the newlywed couple through the grace of God. This flower of love will begin to blossom. You must protect it, water it, and keep it fresh; do not let it wilt and do not neglect it. If you do this, it will remain fresh and full of vigour. As Rumi says, "love turns thorns to flowers." This is exactly how it is.

The most important thing that keeps the family structure strong and lively is love. Love is the cement of any relationship. The fundamental mortar that holds the family together and keeps its foundation strong is love, love, love. Hence, you must keep this love alive. Love is something that needs to be protected; it will not endure on its own. So protect it. A woman needs to kindle this love in her husband's heart and the husband must nurture this love in his wife's heart. The only real way to do this is by being pleasant, united, and honest with one another in life. Be faithful to one another. When a husband and wife are faithful to each other, it creates love, and when this love is present, everything else falls into place.

No one is flawless and there is no perfect spouse on the face of the earth. Therefore, do not magnify each other's flaws. When there is love in the equation, it can cover any flaw that a person can find in another. It will prevent small matters from becoming amplified into large problems. Both husbands and wives should know that the key to increasing and deepening the love between them lies within their own hands. They can deepen their love everyday with good manners and kind behaviour, with intelligence and diplomacy, and with proper interactions. There is no such thing as too much love between a man and his wife. One of the places where there is no limit to this love is between a husband and wife. The more you love one another, the more trust it will bring about between you. Such a love between a husband and wife is actually God-given and desirable. The more it increases, the better it is.

Importance of Trust

However, like anything else, love must be protected and guarded. It is not something that a person can leave unattended for years and expect to find it as he left it. You must keep this love fresh and alive. That which binds a family together is love. It truly transforms life into a source of peace. That is why you must desire it; hence, if your spouse shows affection, reciprocate this affection, and do so genuinely from the depth of your heart. The best way to nurture love in the family is by creating trust between you and your spouse. Try and earn your spouse's trust, and you spouse will feel more comfortable around you and more at ease. In return, you should trust your spouse as well and rest assured. When each spouse manages to gain the other's trust, the love between them will increase day by day. In contrast, when there is no trust between spouses, the very foundation of love becomes weak and unstable.

The veil and sacred boundaries that Islam has put between men and women are in place for this very reason. The husband and wife should feel that the emotional, sexual, and passionate attraction that exists between them must remain exclusively between them; neither of them should seek it in a third party outside of the marriage. Only then will this trust be formed in its full and complete sense.

So when Islam keeps insisting on lowering your gaze

and when it prescribes certain things for women and other things for men, it is because the gaze which you direct on another individual is actually a part of your spouse's share that you have deprived them of. It matters not whether you are a man or a woman; with that gaze, you have transferred a share outside of the marriage and now there is something missing within the marriage. The love between you will weaken and with this, the very foundation of the family will be in jeopardy. You have sold that which you need in exchange for that which will harm you.

In the family, the foundation of love is trust. If a husband and wife lose their trust in one another—for example, if the wife suspects her husband of lying to her or if the husband suspects the same of his wife—and both of them feel that the other is not being genuine in their expressions of love, the foundation of this love will weaken. If you wish for the trust to remain, you must learn to trust in one another. It entails affability, cordiality, observing etiquette, and observing the legislated bounds and limits of religion. Do not let this love dissipate; do not be indifferent to it; protect this love. Indeed, love is God-given but preserving it and increasing it lies in our hands.

The parents of the spouses play an important role in increasing this love; the parents of each spouse should encourage their son or daughter to love their partner. For example, if they see something they disapprove of in their daughter-in-law or son-in-law, they should not be so quick to mention it to their child. Rather, they should leave it for the couple to sort out their own problems as a way of becoming closer and more intimate day by day. When love is strong, everything becomes possible—with love, you can correct bad habits, you can correct irreligiosity, you can overlook faults, and you can mutually enjoin the good and forbid the evil. All problems can be solved with love.

How can one ensure that love endures? How can a wife ensure that she keeps her husband's heart? It is by earning his trust, letting him feel reassured that she is faithful with what he has entrusted her—i.e., his secrets, his close ones, his reputation, and his possessions. And how can a husband ensure that he keeps his wife's heart? It is in the same way, and it is by respecting her. It cannot be a superficial or ceremonial respect, but a genuine one. Genuine respect does not mean you end up calling each other with formal titles; rather, it means that the husband harbours a sense of respect for his wife in his heart and that the wife harbours a sense of respect for her husband in her heart likewise.

A Covering for One Another

A man must never feel he can disrespect or ignore his spouse just because he is faithful to her. For example, if the husband comes home late because he has been outside of the home spending time with his friends, relatives, and acquaintances, while the wife has been at home, alone, either eating by herself or tired, or waiting to have a meal with her husband, this is called neglecting your spouse. If love is snow, then this kind of behaviour will melt it. Similarly, if the wife leaves her husband at home while she spends time conversing with her sister or having fun at a friend's gathering, while he is sitting at home waiting for her—or if they have a child, he is left looking after them for several hours—and she is completely unconcerned about him—about his food, his clothing, etc.—then this can also destroy love.

Be mindful and avoid doing anything that may cause resentment or weariness to grow between you. Find out what your spouse is highly sensitive to and refrain from provoking them in that regard. Some people are completely unmindful about this. For example, a man could have a habit that really annoys his wife but he persists in it, unconcerned about his wife's feelings about it. This is harmful for the relationship. Similarly, a woman may often put her own wants—i.e., for them to buy a certain product, or go to a certain place, etc.—over her husband's comfort and peace. Does this have more priority over the marriage? The most important thing is the relationship between the two individuals; everything else in the world is secondary. Look after one another and be considerate to each other.

Love is not a mountain that will remain on its own; it needs to be protected. It is like a flower—it must be cared for, watered, and nurtured. As long as love endures, the family ambience will be pleasurable. Strive to ensure that your children are nurtured in an atmosphere of mutual love and purity.

At the same time, do not compromise on principles. Do not allow your spouse or your child to break a law, to sin, to be immoral, or to spread corruption. Of course, these matters must not be addressed in a rash and reckless manner; rather, with the help of wisdom and prudence, try to remove each other's shortcomings. If you can do this, life will bloom, future generations will be rectified, and order will be established. These lives will remain and will not be destroyed.

The Qur'ān describes the husband and wife as clothing for one another:

$$هُنَّ لِباسٌ لَكُم وَأَنتُم لِباسٌ لَهُنَّ$$

... they are a garment for you, and you are a garment for them ... (Baqarah, 2:187)

Men are clothes which cover their wives and women are clothes which cover their husbands. What is the purpose of clothing? Clothes have many uses: they protect man, they beautify him, and they cover his defects. When a man is clothed, if he has any defects on his body, they will be covered. Moreover, clothing will adorn a man, protect him from heat and cold, and prevent a stranger from seeing parts of his body that they are not permitted to see. Now, a husband and wife have exactly the same relationship with one another—they must be an adornment, a protector, a preserver, and a *maḥram* for each other. Hence, for a man or woman to reveal the secrets of each other to their friends or neighbours is unacceptable. For them to abuse each other's trust is unacceptable. This is not fidelity.

Each side must trust the other and gain the other's trust through their own actions. They must adorn each other and cover each other's defects. There are some who take every opportunity to complain about their spouse—"he did this" or "she said that." Even if your spouse has a defect, do not expose it to everyone indiscriminately. Each one of you is a garment, a covering, a protector, an adornment, and a source of dignity for the other. If you abide by this, your life will be fruitful. If you find that your life is unsettled, perhaps it is because you have fallen short on these matters. Of course, this is not to say that they are always both to blame; however, it is often the case that both partners do have a share in the blame. Nevertheless, if you are vigilant, your life will be pleasant and the family habitat will become a safe haven.

If a woman feels a sense of psychological and moral security within the house; if she experiences comfort and *sakan* (tranquillity); if her husband has truly become a garment for her as she is a garment for him; if there is love and mercy between them as the Qur'ān has encouraged; if the Qur'ānic injunction of "the wives have rights similar to the obligations upon them" (Baqarah, 2:228) is implemented; if all of these foundational principles exist, then the difficulties outside of the house will become easier for a woman to bear. In fact, she will triumph over such difficulties. If a woman can reduce the difficulties in her own refuge and fort, she will undoubtedly be able to do so in society as well.

Keeping Each Other on the Heavenly Path

The family household is a place of cooperation, and the couple needs to help and support one another in it. This does not mean that a wife has to do her husband's paperwork or that the husband should put on an apron and go to work in the kitchen. These forms of assistance may be very helpful but they fall short of the ultimate target. The greatest support that a husband and wife can offer one another is to help each other stay on the path of God. They must assist each other in preserving their faith and protecting the well-being of one another, both in thought and in practice. Each spouse should become a spiritual sentry for the other and keep watch over them, not like a spy or informant, but like a true guardian angel. There are times when God's angels protect His servants and pray for their forgiveness and this is precisely how a couple needs to be.

Individuals must work towards attaining true human perfections on the path of God, which include proximity to God (*taqarrub ilā Allah*), becoming qualified by His qualities (*takhalluq bi akhlāq Allah*), purifying the soul (*tahḍīb al-nafs*), and becoming transformed into light (*nūr*) on the plane of this earth.

$$لِمِثلِ هٰذا فَليَعمَلِ العامِلونَ$$

Let all workers work for the like of this! (Sāffāt, 37:61)

Not only should they strive for these perfections, but they should assist others in attaining them also.

This is a long journey and one fraught with danger and obstacles. Even though it is the straight path, there are many channels towards it. One cannot undertake this journey by simply wishing it; rather, one must embark upon it with one's heart, one's determination, one's effort, and one's action.

Sisters, help your husbands in this regard. If, for instance, he is studying to acquire knowledge that can be beneficial to other people, then help him with this task. If he wishes to do a good deed, stand beside him. If he is struggling for a just cause and the truth, then be swift in aiding him. If he is striving to strengthen his faith, assist him. If he wants to go on a spiritual retreat (*i'tikāf*), support him. If he is required to take a necessary trip or difficult assignment, then be there for him.

A woman can prevent her husband from being hurled

into the precipice of hell. Whether it is within the household, the workplace, the economic market, or the political arena, a man can stumble and make mistakes. These mistakes can gradually take him to the edge of a cliff, and with one act of negligence, he can tumble to the bottom of the precipice. But a woman can prevent this from happening. When a woman senses that her husband is in difficulty at his workplace or anywhere outside of the house—and many times, women are able to sense this regardless of whether it is financial, political, etc.—it behoves her to help him so that he may overcome his challenges. This is only possible with cordiality, advice, and appropriate words. We know of many women who, in this way, have taken their husbands from the edge of hell to the gates of heaven. Husbands can also do the same—they can prevent their wives from falling into such predicaments. So protect each other, and be persistent in the path of God. Encourage each other towards God-wariness, worship, sincerity, trustworthiness, purity, modesty, and good deeds.

Some men earn a living from illicit sources. When a wife finds out about this, she should use her tactful feminine abilities and elegance to persuade her husband against this type of illicit income. A woman can easily ascertain when her husband has diverted from the straight path in financial, economic, work-related, political, or moral matters. She can do this by reading the signs. A man can do the same in relation to his wife as well. It is then that a moral barrier needs to be erected; this does not mean that one must start a fight or use harsh words. Rather, like a caring nurse or doctor, one must ensure that the family does not fall victim to this plight.

Unfortunately, there are times when the opposite happens—the man may not be inclined to earn an illicit income, but his wife may pressure or force him into doing so.

Sisters, do not let your husbands embark on the path of sin and immorality, and if they have already done so, do not let them continue on that path. At the same time, when you see your husbands doing the right thing, help and encourage them. Brothers, when you see that your wives are serving the community, educating themselves, spreading the faith, or focusing on their supererogatory prayers, encourage and assist them. There are women who pave the way towards heaven for their husbands as there are women who pave the way towards hell; likewise, there are men who pave the way towards heaven for their wives as there are men who pave the way towards hell. When we advise the couple to help and protect each other, we mean that they should make one another deserving of heaven.

"A believer is a believer's compeer."[9] They are counterparts to one another. The faith that lies within them is everything to them. If your faith is less than your spouse's is, you must increase it; if your spouse's faith is less than yours is, you must help them with theirs. If your spouse does not know how to pray, if they do not give importance to prayer, if they are unmindful of ablution and ritual purity, if they are over-focused on external appearances, if they are extravagant, if they are lacking in moral fibre, or if they are tainted with a particular vice, then it is binding on you to help them reform and rectify them. In fact, you can be more effective in this regard than others. A decent young woman who is modest

---

[9] *Al-Kāfī*, vol. 5, "Bāb anna al-muʾmin kufw al-muʾmin".

and strong in her faith can influence her husband to a large degree. Now some women use this influence to direct their husbands' wealth towards purchasing clothing, furniture, or useless objects, while others utilize this same influence to incline their husbands' hearts towards God, and to direct their wealth towards charity, humanitarian aid for the needy, public welfare, and community affairs. Similarly, a young man has considerable influence over his wife, often more so than her father, mother, sister, brother, or teacher.

Advise and protect each other. A woman should be vigilant—if she senses that her husband is deviating from the path of God, she should prevent this with her kind words, deeds, and good counsel. A man should be the same in relation to his wife. This 'protection' can only be achieved through love, cordial words, proper logic, and wise interaction; it cannot be attained through harshness or force. Protect each other in the way of God and encourage one another towards truth and patience. Be an exemplar in your family of the following verse:

$$\text{وَتَوَاصَوْا بِالْحَقِّ وَتَوَاصَوْا بِالصَّبْرِ}$$

and enjoin one another to [follow] the truth, and enjoin one another to patience. (al-ʿAṣr, 103:3)

Not only must the man advise his wife to follow the truth, to be patient, and to persevere in the path of God, but the woman must also counsel her husband to follow the truth, to be patient, and to persevere in the path of God. If a young, believing, reverent, revolutionary, and modest woman decides to act according to this verse—i.e., if she advises her husband to be God-wary, to abstain from self-indulgence, and to live by God's pleasure—this will certainly be much more influential on her husband than anything or anyone else. This advice will have more of an effect on him than any other advice as long as it is said with words of love and affection. It will have an effect on the children as well.

Marriage: A Spiritual or Material Transaction

Marriage is a spiritual, immaterial, and cordial transaction. It is not like a financial transaction that involves funds, cheques, or bank drafts; rather, it is a transaction between hearts and souls. As such, one should not emphasize the financial or material aspects of it, because these aspects can destroy life. The foundation of marriage is a human affair, not a material one. According to Imām Zayn al-ʿĀbidīn (ʿa), wealth can be enchanting: "erase from their hearts the thought of enchanting possessions."[10] It is like a geometric progression—the more that wealth increases, the exponentially greater is its seductive power. Hence, a man must have full control over himself so that his wealth does not consume him, as it so often does. We should not let this seductive wealth make its way into the arena of love, affection, and the exchange of hearts. Some people demand an extremely high dowry; in effect, they have turned this human affair of marriage into a business deal or commercial transaction. This degrades and abases the human value of marriage and is completely unacceptable.

There are some individuals that turn marriage—which

---

[10] Supplication no. 27 of the al-Saḥīfah al-Sajjādiyyah. This is a supplication for the people of the frontiers.

is a human, affectionate, and conscientious affair—into an opportunity for showing off. They say in a flaunting manner, "our daughter's marriage gift included these items; what about yours?" Or, for example, they brag about the venue of the wedding ceremony. This is nothing but vain rivalry. It produces nothing but error upon error. Not only are we tainting the marriage with materialism, but we are also transforming this pure and delicate moment into an arena of ostentation, extravagance, and vainglory. Consequently, the newlyweds now feel they should base their marriage on opulence and ostentation. Why do we do this? Let the newly married couple become habituated to a modest and balanced life from the beginning. Opulence is harmful to society as a whole. People do not disagree with materialism because they are not aware of its enjoyments, but because they know the detriment it causes to society. They see it as a toxic pill or substance and they know that society will suffer from an excess of it. In moderation, there is no problem with enjoying material possessions, but when it turns into rivalry and the idea of keeping up with the Joneses, it has transgressed those bounds and has entered into another arena, thus causing harm to society. So for us to bring this toxic culture into the environs of marriage is far more detrimental.

Some individuals regard the bride's marriage gift or the groom's dowry as a type of investment; they ask her family what marriage gift they will be providing, or when a man proposes, they ask him what dowry he is offering. It is as if they are doing some kind of business transaction or exchanging goods! This sort of attitude is completely unacceptable. Marriage is a human affair, a transaction of the hearts, and an exchange of emotions. The more it contains of spirituality, the greater benefit it will bring to the new family.

Islam has ordained a dowry for marriage, but this is not in order to debase marriage and turn it into a business transaction. There is no exchange taking place here, because both parties are investing in something that belongs to them both. Marriage is not like a purchase or exchange where you give one thing in return for another. Nothing is given nor taken; rather, both parties are investing themselves in something shared between them, for their mutual benefit. This is what marriage is all about.

Material considerations should play a minimal role in all of this, which is why we say a women's dowry should not be too high. In Islam, the dowry is a necessary condition of the marriage contract, but it should be a moderate amount. The reason I have said that we should not make the dowry more than fourteen gold coins is because I want to make this point. From a jurisprudential point of view, a marriage contracted with fifteen, sixteen, or even one thousand gold coins is completely valid. There is no problem in it. Some people have said three hundred and thirteen gold coins is the limit, in an effort to make it religiously symbolic. We say that even if you set your dowry at 124,000 gold coins—the number of all the prophets ever sent to mankind—your marriage contract will still be valid; however, one cannot overlook the other problems that will arise as a result. The newlyweds will face greater problems in society and within their own family. I wanted to set a limit for the dowry so that families would stop vaunting the amount of dowry they received. When I emphasized the limit of fourteen gold coins and warned against ostentation, many people nodded their heads in approval; yet a handful, perhaps lacking in foresight, do not seem to pay any heed, to their own detriment. Their actions do not affect me; rather, they are causing injury to their own selves.

Unfortunately, there are some individuals who use up every opportunity that life has given them in showing off and competing with others. They lie in wait for others to make a move; if the other takes one step, they take two. In marriage, for example, they feel that they must set their daughter's dowry slightly higher than what other people have set their daughter's dowry at, precisely like at an auction! Some people have taken up this custom, and it is not right. If life was all about competing, then many households would lose in this competition.

Moreover, those who think that setting their daughter's dowry high is a form of respect to her are wrong as well; in fact, this is a form of disrespect because they are reducing the 'commodity' in this human transaction—i.e., one of the two 'commodities' of this human transaction—to the level of mere merchandise. It is as if they are putting a monetary value to their daughter. No amount of money can compensate your daughter's worth! Those who assume that a low dowry would weaken their daughter's marriage are also mistaken; if a marriage is based on love and correct principles, it cannot be shaken even if it is devoid of a dowry. Conversely, if a marriage is founded on malice, guile, dishonesty, and deceit, no matter how high the dowry is, an evil, oppressive husband will find a way to avoid paying it. No dowry, no matter how high, can prevent a divorce. What prevents a divorce are one's morals and actions, as well as abiding by the teachings of Islam.

In the early days of Islam, the Prophet (ṣ) entered the mosque and announced that a girl with particular qualities was looking for a husband. He asked if anyone would like to offer his hand in marriage to her. A young man stood up and said, "I would like to." The Prophet (ṣ) asked him what dowry he would offer. He informed the Prophet (ṣ) that he would offer something to the value of a bunch of dates or a basket of dates. The Prophet (ṣ) accepted this dowry on behalf of the girl, performed their marriage contract at that moment, introduced him to his spouse, and told them, "Now you may go home."

This may explain the words of Imam Ḥusayn (ʿa) where he is reported to have said, "The dowry we sought on behalf of our daughters and sisters or the dowry we agreed to with our wives was the dowry of the Prophet (ṣ) (*mahr al-sunnah*)." This was not because they did not have the financial means; if Imam Ḥusayn (ʿa) wanted to contract a marriage with a dowry of one thousand dinars, he could have done so. He did not need to limit his marriage dowry, for instance, to 500 dirhams (12.5 *awqiyyah*[11]). Even though they could have raised the dowry, they chose not to for a particular reason; this is how Islam envisions marriage. The ostentation and particular ways of conducting the marriage that came about in later years are just embellishments created out of human ignorance. They do not have any proper sensible roots. I earnestly request all of the people of this country to avoid raising the dowry for it is a custom based on ignorance. It is something that neither

---

[11] An amount of money equivalent to forty dirhams.

God nor the Prophet (ṣ) are pleased with, particularly in this day and age. I am not saying that it is forbidden by Islam or that it invalidates the marriage contract; what I am saying is that it goes against the customs of the Prophet (ṣ), the Imams (ʿa), and the great Islamic scholars.

The same principle applies to the marriage gift, except that this factor is out of my control; it is entirely in your hands. Be vigilant about this. If someone has the money, there is a strong temptation to add things to their daughter's marriage gift and it is not very difficult to justify the additional expense. Unfortunately, there are some people who, despite not having the adequate funds, still put themselves and their families through great difficulties, sometimes burdening themselves with tremendous amounts of debt in order to prepare a good marriage gift. Why do the girls' families put themselves through such difficulties in order to prepare the marriage gift? And they do not just suffice themselves with any gift, but rather go searching for extravagant and expensive ones—things that are absolutely unnecessary and redundant. It seems that the only motivation is to impress others and to ensure that their marriage gift is no less than the one received by this family member, or that neighbour, or this friend. At times, it is because the father wishes to please his daughter. But he should know that there are other ways to please her while still ensuring a modest marriage gift. A marriage gift is only supposed to cover the couple's basic needs in order to allow them to start a life together. The rest is up to them and they should work it out together with God's help; it is not the parents' responsibility.

There are many individuals that really stretch

themselves, not only to provide a comprehensive marriage gift for their daughter, but also to ensure that it includes the most expensive or fashionable brands. They actually oblige themselves for this task, trying to get everything they can, including the latest and newest products. What is the need for all this? It is a serious mistake. The bride and groom are only two people who want to start a life together and to live like everyone else. If you have the means, you can buy a fridge for the new couple; if you do not have the means, you do not need to buy it. It should not reach the point where you end up looking everywhere, in almost every store, to find things for the marriage gift.

Sisters, do not allow for this. Even if your parents insist on it, do not let this take place. What will you do with all these expensive products and appliances? If you wish to go shopping for the marriage gift and the ceremony, there is no need to go to the most classy areas of the city that are known for carrying the most expensive products. Suffice yourselves with the average stores. Moreover, let it not come to the point where the groom is also dragged into this in order to buy things for the marriage and the bride; unfortunately, this is also being done.

This, in no way implies that marriage gifts should not be provided for the new couple; it is a necessity after all. What is wrong is making it extravagant and going to extremes, particularly if it entails that the bride's family will have gone beyond their means thereby falling into hardship as a result. This is simply unacceptable.

A large dowry and an extravagant marriage gift does not make a girl more fortunate nor does it grant a family the peace, tranquillity, and comfort that it requires. These are life's luxuries and excesses, and have no real benefit. Rather, they only increase us in worries and agitation, at times going beyond this to actually create crises. Hence, it is better to cut down these things as much as possible.

A New Life of Simplicity

Let not the foundations of your new life be based on extravagance. Take the reins of your life and govern it with simplicity and frugality. Now when I say simplicity, this is not to suggest that beauty or beautification is a bad thing; Islam has no objection to beauty, beautification, or anything that can create a pleasant environment for the human soul as long as it does not lead to waste, extravagance, excess, or ostentation. Do not enslave yourselves to formalities. Once you enter the arena of formalities, there is no turning back. There are some people who make life difficult for themselves by being overly concerned with appearances and formalities. The type of clothing, housing, furniture, display items, furnishings, etc. that they choose only makes it difficult for them to keep up with that standard. If they wished, they could have avoided this predicament. Start from now, as you are getting married, to choose a simple, modest, and sufficient life. Live your lives in a way that will make God happy. Make use and take benefit from all the good things that God has created, but make sure that you do so with moderation and justice. Both of these are important. This means being fair and considering how other people are living too. Do not create gaps between yourselves and other people.

Be content with what you have, and do not feel

ashamed by this contentment. There are those who assume that contentment is only for those who are poor or less fortunate and that if you have wealth, you do not need to practice contentment. This is not true. Contentment is when a man stops at what he needs. A life of formalities, a life of ostentation, a life of aristocracy, a life of excessive spending, and a life of extravagance can bring about misfortune. One should live a life of sufficiency and comfort, not wastefulness or excess. Why is it that some people confuse the two? Sufficiency means not to depend on others but to manage one's life without having to rely on them.

High material expectations can straiten one's life and lead to depression; if a person lowers his expectations in life, he will find felicity. This is not only beneficial for the Hereafter, but also for the life here in this world. I advise all of you young, believing women against falling into the trap of consumerism that the West has spread like a disease across the globe, including even developing nations such as ours. God's curse be on those who imported the immoral and alien cultural practices of the West and who shook the very foundations of married life that existed within our own culture and which were derived from Islam itself. They preoccupied our young men and women with formalities and ostentation. Spending should be based on what is necessary, not what is excessive.

The Importance of Accommodating Each Other

A key point to focus on is that the foundation of a good

marriage is that both parties get along with each other. They must learn to work together. This kind of 'getting along' has a very deep meaning. Once, I went to see Imam Khomeini (r) as he was about to solemnize a couple's marriage. As soon as he saw me, he asked me to recite one part of the marriage formula. Contrary to what we usually do, he solemnized the marriage first. Then, instead of giving a long sermon about marriage, he uttered a few words of advice to the newlyweds. He turned to the couple and said, "Go and accommodate each other." At the time, I thought to myself how we normally give such long talks and yet here the Imam summarized all of it in a single sentence—"Go and accommodate each other."

My advice to you is the same: Go and accommodate each other. Let your efforts, particularly during the first phase of your life, be directed towards working together. Live with one another, long for each other, and show love to one another.

Do not have high expectations of each other. Your spouse is not an angel, free from all faults, vices, and deficiencies, so do not expect this of them. We have this tendency when we are young—to paint an image of the ideal spouse in our minds. But this person does not exist, neither in this city nor in this country nor anywhere on this planet. This ideal image of a spouse—free from any fault or blemish—simply does not exist. All of us have our faults and this is just part of being human. We may be immune from one particular fault but there will be other faults lurking within us. Ultimately, we are flawed creatures and this applies to all of us.

Now, as long as we are far from each other, we are blissfully unaware of these faults. However, as soon as we marry and find ourselves living together, these defects begin to surface. Are we going to resent this? No, we must accept life as we find it and work with it. One thing we must definitely not do when we see flaws and imperfections in our partner is to make those flaws bigger than they really are and let ourselves be resentful or miserable about them. Human beings are complex creatures; having negative traits is part of being human as is having positive traits. Of course, there are some flaws which we can overcome and we should; but there are others—physical or psychological—that cannot be corrected. We must live with these flaws and realize that, ultimately, a man's worth is based on how conscious and wary he is of God (*taqwā*). Both partners must try and increase their God-wariness and raise themselves due to it. If one is able to raise oneself due to their God-wariness, this is a distinction. Let the husband and wife assist each other in this race to attain God-wariness.

If you discover a flaw in your spouse tomorrow, do not say to them, "oh, you have a defect!" Every spouse in the world has a defect. A man must know that every woman in the world has a flaw and there is no woman who is flawless. A woman must also know that every man in the world has a flaw. The only exception to this rule are the Infallibles (ʿa) who are preserved from such flaws.

Flaws can be large or small, but in either case, we must accommodate them. These flaws must be acknowledged wherever we find them—in our interactions, in our family lives, and in our social lives. As mentioned, no man is without flaws except for the Infallibles (ʿa). Having stated that, if we study the lives of the Imams from a material point of view, we will find that despite the fact that they were the manifestations of all goodness, their lives contained many difficulties, ultimately ending in their martyrdom. Of course, from our perspective, martyrdom is one of the greatest honours and virtues. But from a material point of view, it can be considered a flaw since it means that one's life is unfairly shortened. The point is that you will not find anyone who is completely free of problems. Everyone has problems. So, if tomorrow, you find a problem in your spouse, do not say regretfully, "I wish I had married someone without this problem." Just know that even if you had married someone else, you would have had to deal with a different problem. So accommodate one another and do not give up your love for one another.

When it comes to the family, working together and compromising is not something that should be looked down upon. It is a positive trait; in fact, it is a necessary trait. As much as we say it is bad to compromise with America, with the Zionists, with the oppressors, when it comes to your spouse, it is good to compromise and accommodate each other. Of course, compromising with friends is good too, but the best of compromises is when it is with your spouse. With the enemy, there is no compromise or surrender; but with the spouse, there should be compromise and surrender. A husband and wife should not decide that whatever they say or whatever they like or whatever gives them their individual comfort is the rule. This is not how it should be. They need to follow a model where they are accommodating each other. If you see that you will not get what you want except by giving in, it is better to give in. Naturally, this applies to both parties, but a woman is able to show this to a greater degree due to her soft disposition and more delicate nature. Men should not take this as a green light to do whatever they please, or to make unreasonable demands and expect their wives to accommodate them. Men must be fair and just. Moreover, this does not mean that women must follow their husbands everywhere and agree with him in every matter. No such idea exists in Islam or in the Islamic law.

الرِّجالُ قَوّامونَ عَلَى النِّساءِ

Men are the managers of women ... (al-Nisā, 4:34)

This verse does not mean that the wife must follow her husband in everything. No, this is not what is intended. At the same time, we cannot be like those people who have not only taken on European attitudes but also go further by saying that women should be in control and men should simply follow! This is also incorrect. At the end of the day, a husband and wife are two partners and two companions. At times, the man must be the one to compromise and at times, the woman. At times, one partner must forgo their preferences and at times, the other. If they do this, they will be able to live together. The Islamic Republic is neither the rule of men nor the rule of women; it is the rule of the family.

An uncompromising attitude makes life bitter. God created the husband and wife to bring tranquillity and peace to their shared life, and if they refuse to accommodate each other, it will rob them of their spiritual tranquillity. This is why when you share your life with someone else, working together and making compromises is essential. For the sake of a sweet and serene life, both parties should be willing to accept and be patient with the shortcomings of each other. Islam has provided a set of teachings for people to follow with regards to their family that naturally solves their problems. It tells men to observe certain things and women to observe certain things; if these teachings are followed, no family will fall into ruin. The truth is that most marriages fail because the couple has not followed these teachings. One does not know how to be considerate; the other does not know how to be prudent; one is excessively irascible; the other is lacking in patience. These are all problems—this one's anger is a problem and that one's obstinacy is also a problem. But if they can curb their anger and be considerate with each other's mistakes—in other words, if they can compromise and accommodate each other—then no family will ever fall into ruin.

At the same time, Islam does not trap a couple in a failed marriage. If due to unfortunate circumstances, a couple is unable to make their marriage work and they are not a good match, there is a way open for them and they can separate. However, they should try and accommodate each other as long as they are able to. Neither the husband nor the wife should ever tell their partner, "I am better than you." What does 'being better' even mean? Does it mean that one's father is better than the other's father? This is utter nonsense. Does it mean that one's wealth is more than the other's wealth? This is also nonsense. Islam does not consider wealth to be a sign of superiority. Does it mean that one is more beautiful than the other? Again, this is absurd. Since when has Islam considered beauty to be a criterion of superiority? Does it mean that one is more wary of God than the other? If this really was the case, it would never be expressed in words. Yes, the only criterion for superiority is one's God-wariness (*taqwā*) and religiosity, yet a person who is truly wary of God would never vocalize this. Any person who says, "I am better" or "I am more wary of God" is actually not very wary of God. He is only showing his moral weakness. Hence, it makes no sense for a husband or wife to tell their spouse that they are better. Islam does not accept the idea that just because your father is wealthier or your family is more reputable and has connections to people in power and position that you are somehow superior.

Therefore, work together and accommodate each other. Appreciate what you have been blessed with and consider it God's gift to you. If you do this, God will shower his blessings on you.

MEN & WOMEN:
THE GENDER ISSUE

Gender in Islam

Why should the relationship between men and women become a vulgar fixation all over the earth, such that every so often it overshadows all of the important and essential aspects of life? This is how it is today. In so many places, the issue of gender relations between men and women has become a fascinating obsession and amusing pastime, often to the point of becoming vulgar in many social settings. Due to this, both men and women have been and are being prevented from being active in the social, political, ethical, and spiritual arenas of life. Islam is against this idea; it cannot accept it.

In God's world, men and women are both fundamental elements of the most complete created order. Without either of them, creation would remain incomplete. If people could recognize the correct place for each of these two elements in the natural realm of humanity and then go on to apply this knowledge, the result would be a perfect divine system. In it, every being would be able to offer its own existential contribution the way it should; no talent would remain unused or be wasted; no one would be oppressed; moreover, mankind would reap the benefits of this harmony, cooperation, and appropriate gathering of men and women, leading to ultimate progress as a society.

Men and women each have their own responsibilities. As the poet says:

> *The world is like the features of a face / everything is beautiful when in its proper place*[12]

When we look at a beautiful face, we cannot say which feature—whether the eyes, lips, nose, or cheeks—contributes more to its beauty; but if any of these features are absent, the face will lose its beauty. The beauty of a face lies in having them all in their proper place. Likewise, everything in this world is part of a perfect divine order. Men and women are no exception to this. When either of them is out of place, the very face of mankind could become incomplete, repulsive, inexpressive, or abhorrent. Neither gender has the right to consider itself more important or valuable than the other. Within this worldview, everyone is on the same plane and

---

[12]Maḥmūd Shabistarī, *Gulshan-i Rāz*.

has one role in the cycle of human life—that one role is to perform one's duty in order to complete the existential world and the life of mankind on it. This is the responsibility of everyone involved—men and women alike—and it entails looking essentially at human beings from the perspective of the divine wisdom that went into the creation of the two genders.

Islam's perspective on gender is that it is a secondary matter. What is primary or essential is the humanity of a person, which is not affected by gender. It is the human being, rather than the man or the woman, whom God addresses. Now, the Qur'ān often addresses the Muslims with the expression, "O you who believe" (yā ayyuha al-ladhīna āmanū), while using the masculine plural instead of the feminine one; but this does not mean that men are given preference over women. The masculine plural is used in this way for reasons which are clear to us, but which we do not wish to discuss in detail right now. It is the same in Persian, when we use mardum to mean "people" even though this word is derived from mard (man). We do not use zanum (from zan meaning "woman") in this way. Likewise, in English, we say human which is from "man". This is not the result of a dominant patriarchal culture that has altered words in a particular way; it has a different reason. Ultimately, in a family, a man represents the external while a woman represents the internal; or to put it more eloquently, we can say that the man is the shell while the woman is its kernel. A man is more apparent by nature; this is how God has created him, just as He created women for other reasons. Therefore, man is more visible and outward because of these qualities and not out of any divine preference for men over women.

In the primary issues that relate to us being humans, there is no difference between the genders. You see this yourself. When it comes to proximity to God, women like Lady Fāṭimah (ʿa), Lady Zaynab (ʿa), and Mary (ʿa) the mother of Jesus (ʿa) have statuses higher than we could possibly imagine. In the chapter of *al-Aḥzāb*, the Qurʾān clearly states that there is no difference between men and women in this regard. Perhaps it was revealed to put an end to this ignorant perspective:

إِنَّ الْمُسْلِمِينَ وَالْمُسْلِمَاتِ وَالْمُؤْمِنِينَ وَالْمُؤْمِنَاتِ وَالْقَانِتِينَ وَالْقَانِتَاتِ وَالصَّادِقِينَ وَالصَّادِقَاتِ وَالصَّابِرِينَ وَالصَّابِرَاتِ وَالْخَاشِعِينَ وَالْخَاشِعَاتِ وَالْمُتَصَدِّقِينَ وَالْمُتَصَدِّقَاتِ وَالصَّائِمِينَ وَالصَّائِمَاتِ وَالْحَافِظِينَ فُرُوجَهُم وَالْحَافِظَاتِ وَالذَّاكِرِينَ اللَّـهَ كَثِيرًا وَالذَّاكِرَاتِ أَعَدَّ اللَّـهُ لَهُم مَغْفِرَةً وَأَجْرًا عَظِيمًا

Indeed the Muslim men and the Muslim women, the faithful men and the faithful women, the obedient men and the obedient women, the truthful men and the truthful women, the patient men and the patient women, the humble men and the humble women, the charitable men and the charitable women, the men who fast and the women who fast, the men who guard their private parts and the women who guard, the men who remember Allah greatly and the women who remember [Allah greatly] - Allah holds in store for them forgiveness and a great reward. (Aḥzāb 33:35)

There is a significant interval and distinction between being a Muslim [in the initial part of the verse] and being one who remembers Allah [near the end of the verse] although the two are linked in a continuous chain. Yet, when a person pays attention to all these words and expressions, he notices that the conclusion—i.e., "Allah holds in store for them forgiveness and a great reward"—applies to both men and women at each stage of that chain: the humble man and the humble woman, the truthful man and the truthful woman, and so on.

In the chapter of *Āl ʿImrān*, God says:

فَاسْتَجَابَ لَهُم رَبُّهُم أَنِّي لا أُضِيعُ عَمَلَ عامِلٍ مِنكُم مِن ذَكَرٍ أَو أُنثىٰ بَعضُكُم مِن بَعضٍ

Then their Lord answered them, 'I do not waste the work of any worker among you, whether male or female; you are all on the same footing ... (Āl Imrān 3:195)

This again shows that there is no difference between men and women.

When it is said that men and women each have specific duties and roles, this does not mean that they do not have mutual duties as well. In fact, the common realm between them is very broad, much broader than their own specific realms. So even though each gender has a specific role to play which the other cannot fulfil—or, at least, cannot fulfil appropriately—there is a very broad realm between the two of them that is common. This realm includes the social, political, and economic life; it includes human development and everything that human beings are capable of doing beyond that which is specific to men or women. This is how we must view men and women in the divine Islamic system. Each gender has its own specific role that it must not forsake, but there is also a wider realm in which both must cooperate, put their talents to use, and not neglect their responsibilities in this mutually shared arena.

Women make up half of the world's population. If one examines this half and compares it to the other, they will realize that this half has the most sensitive, delicate, lasting, and effective role in the history of mankind and its journey towards attaining perfection. This is how God has created women. If we were to divide human activity into two sections—delicate work and hard labour—it would become apparent that delicate work, intricate activity, and the nurturing of emotions one thread at a time is the domain of women.

This is the divine vision regarding men and women. There is a particular aspect in the creation of men and women, which [if misunderstood] can become the basis of deviations, errors, and misguided movements. Unfortunately, this can be seen throughout the centuries and even today. The fact is that men and women are different in terms of their nature—whether it relates to their physical bodies, their emotional constitutions, or the fabric of their spirituality. These differences are related to their ability to perform the particular duties assigned to them and, therefore, play an important role.

The Distinct Roles of Men and Women

These two roles are distinct from one another, but both are indispensable. Merging the two not only goes against nature but doing so, in effect, would be to undermine something that is good. It is like this: Imagine that a professional gardener has carefully arranged a beautiful garden; then we come in and disrupt it based on our own whims, mixing up flowers that have been arranged in a calculated manner.

For a woman, a man is a point of trust and reliance; in fact, that is how a man shows his affection to his wife. So when a woman looks at a man with love and affection, it is in his role as a point of support—someone that she can rely on, someone whose physical and intellectual strength she can make use of in order to move forward in life. However, when a man looks at a woman, he sees her as a symbol of beauty, elegance, tenderness, and comfort. Therefore, man is the point of support in the external aspects of life, while woman is the point of support in the spiritual and emotional aspects of it. A woman is like an ocean of love and affection, and when a man is in her presence, she has the capacity to make him forget his sorrows and distress. These are the God-granted capabilities of men and women. Nature is also like this; it does what it is supposed to but since we do not understand it, we do not respond to it.

At times, a man may remove this capacity and this source of energy from a woman by being bad tempered, forcing her to perform arduous tasks, expecting too much from her, and belittling her. When this happens, the woman can no longer act as that point of comfort—she cannot grant him peace. Instead, she becomes a claimant. A woman could make the same mistake with a man as well; instead of utilizing his stability and perseverance and seeing him as a pivot to rely on, she may deal with him as a mere labourer or even a fool—anything is possible when people make mistakes. Instead of making use of this source of energy and power, she may transform him into quite the opposite. These problems exist but they should not be ignored.

This is what Islam says: The man is a source of strength (*qawām*) while the woman is a source of peace (*rayḥan*). This is neither demeaning to men nor to women. It is neglecting neither the rights of men nor the rights of women. On the contrary, it is taking account of the nature of each gender. In fact, the weight and value of each one is exactly the same. In other words, when you put the gender that represents subtlety, fondness, beauty, and the beautification of the sacred environment of the home on one pan of a scale and you put the gender that portrays leadership, hard work, reliance, and the stronghold of women on the other pan of the scale, you will find the two sides equal. Neither side will outweigh the other.

But today, we have erroneous social currents—not just limited to women but also to men—that wish to exchange the two sides of the scale and reverse the roles. What do they expect from this reversal other than error? What do they expect other than to destroy that beautifully arranged garden? They cannot hope for anything else. They can no longer make use of the genius of each gender. They are undermining the trust within the family environment. They are disorienting both men and women with doubts. They are removing the love and affection, which form the very foundation of the family.

There are times when the man takes on the role of a woman in the house. The woman takes charge and dictates duties to the man, while he submits himself to her commands; this is a kind of relationship seen in some households. In a situation like this, the man can no longer act as fortress of support that a woman needs. At other times, the opposite is the case. The man overworks his wife by getting her to do all the purchasing of the house and coordinating all the activities pertaining to it. This materializes because the man does not have time, and his excuses are, "I have too much work at the university... I have to stay longer in the office... I do not have time... I need to go to work ... etc." The woman is then left with tasks that are tedious and difficult. She may be kept busy with these tasks, but that is not her job!

Islam's View on Women

Islam describes women realistically:

$$\text{فَاِنَّ المَرأَةَ رَيحانةٌ و لَيسَت بِقَهرَمانَةٍ}$$

A woman is a flower, not a chambermaid![13]

Rayḥān means 'flower'. What do we do with a flower? How do we treat a flower? If you wrestle with a flower, you will destroy it. But if you recognize a flower for what it is and treat it accordingly, it will be a source of beauty and influence, and its purpose will become clear.

A woman is "not a chambermaid" (*qahramānah*). *Qahramān* in Arabic does not have the same connotations

---

[13] *Nahj al-balāghah*, letter 31 (Will to Imam Ḥasan on his return from Ṣiffīn)

as in Farsi [which means 'victor']; it is actually an Arabic expression taken from Farsi but it means a 'foreman'—i.e., someone who directly overlooks the work. Therefore, this expression exemplifies the idea that your wife is not your employee and you are not her boss. It should not be assumed that tasks such as raising the children and completing the housework is her job and that the man is in charge of her.

A woman must be treated in accordance with her nature and reality. A woman cannot forget her own nature and most women do not even want to; otherwise, both parties will find themselves in an antagonistic arena. These feminists—which include both men and women—who claim to defend the rights of women, are largely ignorant of what these rights of women are. In my opinion, rights are not arbitrary conventions. All educated people will recognize this. Rights must be sourced in reality. A true right is one that is based on a source that corresponds to the nature of reality. But the rights that these feminists propound have no basis; they are illusionary. Rights that exist for a man and a woman must be supported by their natures—the nature of men and the nature of women or the make-up of men and the make-up of women.

Therefore, if we are to summarize the differences between men and women, we must say that women, in their natural make-up, have more finesse when compared to men. This does not mean they are less resilient. Even experience has shown that women can be just as resilient, if not more so, than men when confronting a variety of physical and material challenges. But women have a type of finesse. Typically, their bodies are smaller and they are emotionally more vulnerable than a man. This is a difference between men and women. Now, if we imagine a scenario of these two creatures living side by side in a lawless place where the rules of wisdom and logic are absent, and we know that one of them is physically stronger, harsher, and taller than the other, and has bigger bones and a deeper voice, while the other is physically weaker, then the outcome is evident. The stronger one will dominate, exploit, harm, and take into service the weaker one. This is an inevitable outcome in a place that lacks any wisdom or law.

Of course, a woman does have certain strengths, tactics, and qualities particular to her that can allow her to overcome a man, but this can only be done through wisdom and prudence. Through her finesse and prudence, a woman can wrap a man around her fingers. We know this is the case through our own experiences and our minds can attest to it as well. It is a fact. Of course, there are some women who are not prudent and hence lack such a power. But a woman who does possess this prudence is able to tame a man to herself in the same way as a person is able to tame a lion. This is not because the person is physically stronger than the lion but because he has managed to use his *inner* strength. Women have this kind of strength through their finesse. When we say finesse, we are not just referring to the finesse of her physical make-up; rather it is a finesse related to her mind, her prudence, and her decisiveness with which God has blessed her.

Nonetheless, in a lawless atmosphere—an atmosphere devoid of wisdom and intellectuality—damage can occur. This damage is when one gender misuses the other, and unfortunately, it has occurred throughout human history from ancient times to the present. The male gender has taken advantage of a lawless and unethical society in order to oppress the female gender. This has happened throughout history and is still happening today. Of course, it is not the case that this has always taken place everywhere; at times, the opposite has actually transpired. There have been places where law and wisdom have reigned, or where the culture of the people did not allow such a thing to materialize. Nonetheless, the majority of lifestyles in the past have been as we have described.

By perusing various books and articles, one can gain an understanding of how certain cultures in the past viewed women or how they treated them. One example of this is provided by the verse of the Qur'ān:

$$\text{وَإِذَا بُشِّرَ أَحَدُهُم بِالْأُنثَىٰ ظَلَّ وَجْهُهُ مُسْوَدًّا وَهُوَ كَظِيمٌ}$$

When one of them is brought the news of a female [newborn], his face becomes darkened, and he chokes with suppressed agony. (Naḥl, 16:50)

It is truly saddening to think of the suffering caused throughout history because of a lack of reason, wisdom, and law. In the jungle, where there is no law or wisdom, can a strong animal control its insatiable desires and appetites for attacking its prey? If we allow our society to become like a jungle, the relations between men and women would be as ugly and bitter as what we have seen in the past, and what we are witnessing, unfortunately, even today.

Anyone who supposes that this does not occur in the West today and that women are not oppressed there just because they speak of the equality between the sexes or of women's rights is gravely mistaken. There are some truly frightening accounts involving oppression and aggression whereby women have been mistreated, whether in the context of work or in other contexts being too shameful to recall. When I saw statistics from one Western country indicating that wife beating was a widespread problem there, I was shocked. The statistics were truly shocking. The article claimed that these were the statistics of just the women who had filed a report. As for how many others exist, who either are overlooked or remain silent due to fear, is unknown. As you can see, the problems faced by women are not solved by the solutions proposed by the West such as condoning scant dressing, encouraging women to leave their homes, distancing them from the *ḥijāb*, etc. Therefore, we must not delude ourselves into believing that by removing or reducing a woman's *ḥijāb*, or by relaxing Islamic rules, the problems that women face will be solved. Not only will we fail to solve these problems, but we will make them far worse.

What Islam strives for is to bring about a fundamental change. Islam attempts to bring about an environment in which the gender which is physically stronger—which, of course, does not imply intellectual or academic strength—does not use this strength to oppress the weaker one. People often relate a narration from Imam ʿAlī (ʿa) to try and attack women and sometimes men too, while that statement was more than likely a reflection of Imam Ali's (ʿa) displeasure regarding the situation he was in. In the same way that we show our resentments today, he was probably doing the same. Nevertheless, just because one gender is physically stronger—and, hence, may have wider bones, a taller stature, and a deeper voice—does that imply that he will also be wiser and have better management skills? Certainly not! Does it mean that he is more capable in the shared ground of politics, economics, education, etc.? No! The reasoning behind this is because these matters depend on participation and hands-on experience.

If, for another thousand years, women are excluded from different aspects of life, then we would continue to see that most of the academics, politicians, entrepreneurs, and those who are active within the social spheres will be menfolk. However, if men were to be prevented from such activities and if women were to replace them, within a few years, we would find the opposite—women would be more capable and men less capable in those fields. Of course, this is also not right and is a type of oppression. Hence, solving the issue of the two genders and preventing the oppression of one gender over the other is dependent on three factors— all of which are non-material. When they are brought into the equation, the material factors will lose their authority. By material factors, we mean taking recourse in one's outward strength. These and other material factors will subside the moment that non-material factors are introduced.

One of these three non-material factors is law, which should be designed to prohibit oppression. Another factor is raising the intellectual level of women through education and a variety of academic, social, economic, literary, and artistic activities. Even now, most of the illiterate are women. We must struggle against this in order for our women to develop their intellects and their practical skills so that they do not become the target of oppression. If women are able to develop themselves through literacy, awareness, management, and wisdom, it will prevent oppression through physical dominance. However, literacy and education is not always the critical factor; what is crucial is wisdom. There are many cases where people are very educated but they lack wisdom and practical skills. The opposite is also possible, of course. Hence, what is important is that women gain the necessary degree of wisdom and practical skill so as to prevent oppression stemming from physical dominance and neutralize it.

A culture of spiritual and ethical education should be made popular amongst women themselves. They must take it upon themselves to think about these issues. They need to focus more on knowledge, on information, on studying, and on the fundamental questions of life. In fact, during the era of despotism in Iran, it was due to the negative influence of Western culture that women began to focus on cosmetics, vanity, ostentation, and flaunting themselves in public. All this, of course, was a sign of the rule of men. In the West, one of the signs that men are in control, is that they want women for their satisfaction; hence, they encourage them to dress up because it gives them pleasure! This is a form of male control, not female freedom. If anything, it is freedom for men! They want the freedom to take pleasure in seeing women, which is why they encourage a woman to cast aside her coverings and beautify herself publically for them. This is a kind of selfishness that many men who lived in irreligious societies displayed in the past and continues to this day. The West is the clearest example of this. Therefore, the imperative for women to educate themselves through knowledge is something that women need to take seriously and give it importance.

The third factor is that we must increase the general intellectual level of society as a whole. In a society where people possess a higher level of intellectual awareness, thoughtfulness, and wisdom, it is evident that they do not abuse each other as much as when this is not the case.

The Importance of Hijab

Islam has considered all things with wisdom when accounting for the issue of *ḥijāb*. The more that it is analysed, the greater the depth that is discovered. Islamic law has clearly stated the parameters of *ḥijāb* and it is important to be aware of them; there is no need to overstep these parameters and go to either extreme. Women in Iran have a good form of *ḥijāb* but, of course, it is not the only form of *ḥijāb*. There are many Muslims all over the world with their own unique styles of *ḥijāb* different from the Iranian *chādor*. In our opinion, the *chador* is definitely good and one of the best forms of *ḥijāb*. Whoever devised it—in the form that appears in this country—has come up with a decent form of covering.

Nonetheless, the most important issue is the *ḥijāb* itself and we need to understand what it means. *Ḥijāb* is not the idea of women covering themselves from men; it is that which lies between the private domain of men and women.

Women merely practice it in one way and men in another. A woman's finesse, as we alluded to before, places special responsibilities on her shoulders. Imam Ali ('a) says, "A woman is a flower." This wonderful description expresses the finesse and elegance of a woman very well. There is no expression stating, "A man is a flower." But being a flower automatically bestows upon a person certain responsibilities that must be observed.

Observing *ḥijāb* is not meant to limit women in any way, shape, or form from academic or political activities. The proof of this is the number of women who observe *ḥijāb* whilst being scholars, students, and participating members in politics and society, as well as many other fields. *Ḥijāb* is not an obstacle for them. It has never been the case in our society that those women who do not observe proper *ḥijāb* have been innately more successful, whether in education or in any other area in general. Even when the previous regime encouraged women to take off their *ḥijāb*s, we did not see that those women who did so were any more successful or better educated than those who did not. In fact, it was quite the opposite; those who were better educated and more skilled voluntarily chose to avoid living in that way. We see the same situation today.

Hence, on the one hand, this particular Muslim covering called the *ḥijāb* is not a barrier for women who want to develop themselves in any field, whether material or spiritual. On the other hand, the prevalence of *ḥijāb* within a society brings about irreplaceable benefits for women in it. One of these benefits is protecting the foundation of the family which, without the practice of *ḥijāb*, is difficult to do.

This is an issue that Western society is currently facing.

This is not to say that only those families where *ḥijāb* is practised are the ones that result in a loving family environment. Such an environment can be created even without the *ḥijāb*. We do not say that wherever *ḥijāb* is not practiced, the family is necessarily on shaky grounds. Rather, if a social environment lacks the concept of *ḥijāb*, this would naturally erode the position of the family and this is what has resulted in the West.

This issue has subsequent consequences that can, at times, be overwhelming for a society. It includes the weakening of the family and the lamentable statistics regarding the trafficking of women. According to a report—ostensibly from the United Nations or some central body—one of the fastest growing businesses in the world today is the trafficking and smuggling of women. One of the worst countries in this regard is the Zionist regime. With the pretext of employment or marriage, girls and women are gathered together from poverty-stricken countries such as Latin America, parts of Asia, and poor European countries and are then delivered to certain establishments where they experience extremely difficult conditions. Naming these establishments or even thinking about them brings a shiver to the soul. All of this originates from an unjust and incorrect notion of a woman's place and role in society. The appearance of so many illegitimate children, of which America has one of the highest rates, is the result of people co-habiting without getting married. In reality, all of these problems—i.e., destroying the family unit, removing the warmth and intimacy within the family environment, and preventing individuals from benefiting from these blessings—stem from the first problem. A solution has to be found—i.e., the true status of women must be ascertained. We need to counter in a serious manner this empty logic of the West.

I was once asked how I would defend the allegations of the West about the status of women in our country. I answered: We do not need to defend; we need to be on the offensive! It is the West that owes the world an explanation; we are the claimants in this case. It is the West who has oppressed women, belittled them, and denigrated them all in the name of freedom, employment, and giving responsibility. But what they have done is subjugated women to spiritual, psychological, and emotional pressure, tarnishing their status and position. If anyone has to defend his record on women's rights, it is the West, not us.

The West stealthily avoids the issue of family. In all the debates they have, they mention women's issues but they never mention the *family*. This is their weak point. They talk about the rights of women, without mentioning the importance of a family, even though a woman cannot be separated from her family. It is necessary for us to understand this point.

In a lecture that I gave at the United Nations, I spoke for over an hour about the importance of family life. Later, I was informed that even though America is normally very keen to censor my talks, on this occasion they actually focused on my talk about the family and broadcast it several times while commenting on it. This is because I mentioned the subject of the family. For the West today, a message that discusses the subject of the family is like cool, pleasant water; it is quenching precisely because it is what is lacking. The issue of the family is a very sensitive one. Whenever family values are given importance, people pay attention because this is one of the core issues and problems that they are currently facing. This is the state of Western culture today.

In contrast, wherever the *ḥijāb* and modesty is observed completely or even partially, the family unit is generally much stronger. There is a strong correlation between the two. One of the ways in which the *ḥijāb* brings felicity to women is that it prevents some of the abuses towards them that were just mentioned. One of the major issues facing women in places polluted with Western culture and their billboards is the pressure to adorn themselves with makeup and cosmetics before leaving the home, in order to display themselves. This is truly one of the most important challenges. Thankfully, our own religious and revolutionary women are less affected by this, though I do believe that there are those who are tarnishing the purity and sincerity of those earlier days by intentionally directing women towards the same path. However, they are harming themselves by this because focusing on such trivial things wastes their time, energy, and money. If women do not go to extremes in self-beautification, they would have more time, energy, and money to spend on things that are more beneficial to them. This is Islam's viewpoint and it is a sure remedy.

Conceptualizing Women's Freedom

The imperialistic world, immersed in a [new] age of ignorance, is wrong to think that a woman's true value and worth lies in beautifying herself for men, in order for them to cast lustful glances at her and to applaud her out of sheer enjoyment. This exaggerated talk of women's freedom in the world, especially in Western culture, is actually based on having women visually available for men in order to satisfy their lust. Is this what freedom for women means? Does it mean that men derive pleasure from them and they become a source of pleasure for men? Those who claim to support the rights of women in the West—whose civilization has become ignorant and deviated—are, in fact, their oppressors.

Let us view a woman as a noble human being; only then will her perfection, her rights, and her freedom become clear to us. When we see a woman as a person who can bring peace to society by raising noble individuals, then we will truly understand what rights she possesses and what freedoms she must enjoy. Let us look at her role in the family. Even though a family originates with a man and a woman, only a woman and a woman's touch can bring peace and tranquillity to a house. When seen from this angle, how she can pursue perfection and what her rights are become evident.

When the Europeans created new industries—at the onset of the nineteenth century when Western capitalists established large factories—and there was a need for cheap and easy labour, the buzz of women's freedom became audible. This was in order for them to bring women out of their homes and put them to work in these factories, as affordable labour. In this way, they could fill their own pockets at the price of the dignity and respect of a woman. What we see with women's freedom in the West today is a continuation of this same movement. The way in which Western civilization has oppressed women and the distorted picture they have portrayed of women in their culture and literature is unprecedented in the entirety of human history. Undoubtedly, women have been oppressed in all times and places, but this kind of large-scale, pervasive, and multi-faceted oppression belongs only to this latest era of Western civilization.

When women were objectified for the satisfaction of men, it was called freedom for women, whereas, in fact, this was the freedom for wayward men. Women were oppressed, not only in the fields of employment and industry, but in the fields of art and literature as well. A simple survey of stories, novels, paintings, and all manners of artistic work will illustrate clearly how women are portrayed. Has any attention been given to the positive qualities and noble values that exist within a woman? Has there been any focus on those tender emotions and that loving kindness that God has granted women? Have her maternal instincts and caretaking spirit with regard to children been emphasized or have they simply focussed on her sensuality, calling it 'love'? This is not love; it is lust. In general, they wished to create a disposition among women to be consumers, generous spenders, low-maintenance workers, and cheap labourers. Is this what is meant by respect for women?

Apparently, in order to be free, a woman must remove her ḥijāb, dispose of her modesty, and put her body on display for men's enjoyment. Is this honour or humiliation? A West that is negligent and intoxicated has allowed itself to fall under the influence of Zionist groups; they introduce this as women's honour and some people have bought into it. A woman's respect does not lie in her ability to attract the gaze of men or the cravings of the lustful. This is not a source of pride for a woman; it is a source of humiliation. A woman's respect lies in protecting her modesty, which God has placed in her nature. It is to combine this with the honour of being a believing woman; it is to combine this with her sense of duty and responsibility. It is to use her finesse at the right time. It is to use her incisiveness of faith at the right time. This delicate combination only belongs to women—the combination of elegant finesse and incisiveness.

A world where a woman has been distanced from her family, brought out of the house with empty promises, left defenceless against the onslaught of society's gazing eyes and lustful activities, and subjugated to having her rights trampled upon, is a world wherein the woman will be weakened, the family destroyed, and future generations placed in grave danger. Any society or civilization that follows this logic is headed towards disaster; this is what is happening in the world right now and is increasing with each passing day. Heed my words: this is a dangerous storm, the destructive power of which will only be felt in the future; it will destroy the very foundations of Western civilization. In the short-term, we may not see all of its effects, but within a century or two, it will become highly evident. The signs of this ethical crisis in the West have already begun to show themselves today.

Honouring Women

Islam honours women in the true sense of the word. If it emphasizes the role of the mother and her sanctity within the household, or if it emphasizes the role of a woman, her influence, her rights, her duties, and her limitations within the household, it is not in order to prevent her from participating in societal matters and contributing in her nation's struggles. Some people have misunderstood this while others have utilized this misunderstanding for their own self-interest. It is as if a woman can only do one of two things: either be a good mother and spouse or devote herself completely to social activities. Nothing could be further from the truth; a woman must be a good mother and a good wife and still be socially active. Lady Fāṭimah (ʿa) is an exemplar of a woman who combines such different roles. Lady Zaynab (ʿa) is yet another. All the famous and well-known women of early Islam and great women of other times are examples of this truth; these women were active in society.

The problems stem from a misunderstanding of the concept of honouring women in Islam, combined with the incorrect ideas of Western civilization about what it means to honour women. These have come together and given rise to an incorrect intellectual movement. A woman in her family is beloved, honoured, and the pivot of managing domestic matters. She is the candle of her entire family. It is she who brings love, peace, and tranquillity into it. The family, which is the cradle of repose for every individual from the vicissitudes of life, can only provide that repose and peace when the woman is there. To study the role of a woman as a wife, as a mother, and as a daughter in order to elaborate her honourable position would need a lengthy chapter. We really need to revisit and rewrite the issue of women and her value and nobility according to Islam.

In one narration, the Prophet (ṣ) says:

المرأة سيّدة بيتها

A woman is the mistress of her house.[14]

While speaking to an audience of men, he told them that the best of them are those who deal in the best manner with their wives.[15]

These are just a few of Islam's comments regarding the issue and there is no shortage of them. In the Qur'ān, when Allah wants to bring an example of someone who pleases God and of someone who disbelieves in Him, both examples are women. It is very interesting that the Qur'ān chooses women as exemplars of good and evil:

ضَرَبَ اللَّهُ مَثَلًا لِلَّذينَ كَفَرُوا امرَأَتَ نوحٍ وَامرَأَتَ لوطٍ كانَتا تَحتَ عَبدَينِ مِن عِبادِنا صالِحَينِ فَخانَتاهُما فَلَم يُغنِيا عَنهُما مِنَ اللَّهِ شَيئًا وَقيلَ ادخُلَا النّارَ مَعَ الدّاخِلينَ وَضَرَبَ اللَّهُ مَثَلًا لِلَّذينَ آمَنُوا امرَأَتَ فِرعَونَ إِذ قالَت رَبِّ ابنِ لي عِندَكَ بَيتًا فِي الجَنَّةِ وَنَجِّني مِن فِرعَونَ وَعَمَلِهِ وَنَجِّني مِنَ القَومِ الظّالِمينَ وَمَريَمَ ابنَتَ عِمرانَ الَّتي أَحصَنَت فَرجَها فَنَفَخنا فيهِ مِن روحِنا وَصَدَّقَت بِكَلِماتِ رَبِّها وَكُتُبِهِ وَكانَت مِنَ القانِتينَ

---

[14] *Nahj al-faṣāḥah*, ḥadīth no. 2177.

[15] *Biḥār al-anwār*, vol. 68, "Kitāb al-īmān wa al-kufr, abwāb makārim al-akhlāq, bāb 92 - ḥusn al-khalq", ḥadīth 47.

Allah cites an example of the faithless: the wife of Noah and the wife of Lot. They were under two of our righteous servants, yet they betrayed them. So they did not avail them in any way against Allah, and it was said [to them], 'Enter the Fire, along with those who enter [it].' Allah cites an example of the faithful: the wife of Pharaoh, when she said, 'My Lord! Build me a home near You in paradise, and deliver me from Pharaoh and his conduct, and deliver me from the wrongdoing lot.' And Mary, daughter of Imran, who guarded the chastity of her womb, so We breathed into it of Our spirit. She confirmed the words of her Lord and His Books, and she was one of the obedient. (Taḥrīm, 66:10-12)

Here the Qur'ān uses two women as an example for the faithless: the wives of Noah and Lot, two of God's prophets. These two women betrayed their husbands. The issue here is related to the subject of the family. Similarly, the example of the two virtuous women is also related to the family. The first is Pharaoh's wife, who is given great importance and respect because she raised Moses, who was one of God's prophets, in her arms, believed in him, and supported him (which is why Pharaoh took revenge upon her). So as part of her role in the family, she had a great influence on human history by raising someone like Moses. The same applies to Mary "who guarded the chastity of her womb"—i.e., she protected her dignity and modesty. This shows us that at the time in which she was living, there had been threats to the modesty and dignity of chaste women but she had been able to resist these threats. So we can see that all these examples are connected both to a woman's role in the family and her status in society as a whole.

From this, we conclude that the essential building block of a family is a woman, not a man. A family can still function without a man—as when the man of the house passes away or is not present at home; in a situation like this, if the wife is wise and possesses good management skills, she can still maintain her family. Therefore, it is the lady of the house who keeps the family together.

Women and Society

There are, however, some who would strongly oppose what we are saying; they would accuse us of wanting to imprison women in their homes and prevent them from participating in social activities. Nothing could be further from the truth; Islam demands nothing of the sort. Allah says the following in the Qur'ān:

$$\text{المُؤمِنونَ وَالمُؤمِناتُ بَعضُهُم أُولِياءُ بَعضٍ يَأمُرونَ}$$
$$\text{بِالمَعروفِ وَيَنهَونَ عَنِ المُنكَرِ}$$

But the faithful, men and women, are comrades of one another: they bid what is right and forbid what is wrong ... (Tawbah, 9:71)

In other words, believing men and women both play a role in guiding and protecting the community and society as a whole; both must enjoin the good and forbid the evil. Since the Qur'ān [in the verse above] has not excluded women, neither must we. The responsibility for the well-being of

Muslim society, its management, and its continued progress falls on the shoulders of both men and women, each of whom have responsibilities based on their unique abilities. There is no debate over whether women can have responsibilities outside of the house; it is obvious that they can. Islam does not completely negate this possibility. But what we are discussing here is whether a woman has the right to abandon the house and her role in the family unit entirely in order to pursue her desires and ambitions outside the family environment, thereby sacrificing her position as a mother and a spouse! Does she have this right or not? This is the focus of our discussion.

I say that the most important role that a woman could fulfil—regardless of her level of education, knowledge, research, or spirituality—is that role that she would fulfil as a mother and a wife. This is more important than all of her other functions; this is something that no one but a woman can fulfil. If a woman has another important responsibility or task, there is nothing wrong in that; but her role as a mother or as a wife should be her primary and essential responsibility. The very preservation and growth of the human race as well as the development of man's inner faculties is dependent on this; the protection of the spiritual health of a society is dependent on this; peace, comfort, and tranquillity in the face of this world's instabilities, disorders, and agitations are dependent on this. It is not something we can afford to underestimate.

It is not an achievement for a woman to imitate what a man can do; a woman has her own womanly function, the value of which is much greater than any manly function she may perform. Today, there is an anti-value movement spreading around the globe that is fostered by very dubious agents. Unfortunately, our country is no exception to this. The proponents of this movement wish to force women to be men. They consider it degrading for women that men can fulfil certain functions that women cannot. Is this degrading? What an erroneous perspective! They find fault in us for calling a woman 'a woman' and a man 'a man'. But is this not the case? They expect us to say that a woman is a man, a manufactured man, a *copy* of a man! How can this be a source of pride for a woman? A woman's pride is to be a woman, a true woman, a true female. If we look at things from a spiritual point of view, certainly being a true woman is no less valuable than being a true man; on the contrary, at times, it is actually even more valuable. Why would any woman want to give this up?

Of course, there are some responsibilities that are common to both men and women. As we mentioned before, the responsibility for being socially conscious and active, understanding the problems facing the community, and trying to solve these problems is neither exclusive to men nor to women. Even women cannot decide to shed this collective responsibility.

In the early Islamic state, women were active on the battlefield; they were mostly nurses who cared for the injured, but in some of the most difficult battles, they would cover their faces, take up arms, and fight the enemy. These same women would still go home, embrace their children with love, and continue raising them in an Islamic manner. All of this would be done while maintaining their *ḥijāb* and modesty because none of these roles contradicted one another. Some people go to extremes on this issue. On one hand, there are those who say that being socially active prevents women from looking after their families; therefore, women should not take part in social activities. On the other hand, there are those who say that having a family is a hindrance to social participation; therefore, we should forget getting married or having children. Both of these ideas are wrong and neither should be sacrificed to accommodate the other.

When questioned whether women should be allowed to work, I respond to them in the affirmative. We are opposed to women remaining jobless; women should definitely work. However, there are two kinds of work: work inside the house and work outside the house. If a woman has the skills to work outside of the house, she should do so. This is, in fact, very good, but it comes with a condition: this employment—even if it is inside the house—should not be such that it affects the relationship between a husband and wife. There are some women who overwork themselves from morning to night and when their husbands return home, they lack the energy to even smile at them. This is not good. Housework needs to be done, but not to the point of disintegrating the family.

I completely agree that women should work; I agree with all sorts of social activities for women, whether entering into employment, politics, social work, charitable endeavours, etc. All of these are decent preoccupations. Women are half the population and they can contribute tremendously to our society's productivity and development. Nonetheless, there are important principles that should not be overlooked, such as the following: the primary work of a woman which pertains to her home, her family, her spouse, and her role as a mother should not be undermined. There are women who have managed to maintain this balance—of studying, teaching, housekeeping, having children, raising them, etc.—but it has been undoubtedly difficult.

Therefore, as long as the primary irreplaceable task of a woman is not harmed, we are completely in favour of women participating in society. If, as a woman, you decide not to have children at all ... if as a mother, you decide not to raise your children at home ... if you decide not to open up the ever-so-delicate threads of your child's emotions—threads that are finer than silk—with your own fingertips so that they do not get tangled up later in life, then just know that no one else will be able to do this. Even a father cannot do this, let alone anyone else. This feat can only be accomplished by a mother. As for that employment outside the house, if you cannot do it, there will be tens of people to take your place. Hence, the priority must lie with the task that is irreplaceable.

Do not think that this belittles women in any way; on the contrary, it elevates her. The woman is at home managing and preparing the family environment—that place that will nurture a new sapling, a human being—while the man is tasked to go out and perform his work so that he can bring back the nutriments for this habitat. This is how we should conceive of it. Or to take another analogy, imagine a room with two people. One is tasked with managing the room, while the other goes out to gather food since they will need food to survive. Does this division of labour demean either of them? If anything, the one who is tasked with the household duties and is responsible for building this habitat would appear to demand greater respect; it is the man that is in her service. However, when it comes to social responsibilities, resistance, and politics, both men and women need to be present. When the call is made to strive in the way of God, both men and women must do their part.

Before the Islamic Revolution, when we were struggling against the tyranny of the Shah, there were many men who had taken to the streets and were engaged in revolutionary activities, but their wives dissuaded them from this because they were unable to bear the difficulties that accompanied it. In contrast, there were many women who encouraged their husbands to rise against the regime, helped them in this cause, and strengthened them with their emotional support. In 1977 and 1978, when the streets and alleys of Iran were overflowing with people, women played a crucial role in this by supporting their husbands and children and sending them out to demonstrate against the government.

Later, during the Revolution and the subsequently imposed war, mothers turned their sons into brave and dedicated soldiers for the sake of Islam. Wives transformed their own husbands into men of strength and resistance. This is a woman's power over her son and husband. This is the same influence that a woman can have inside her home and within her own family, and it is one of the most important roles a woman can have. In my estimation, this is *the* most important duty a woman could perform—i.e., to raise her children and to strengthen her husband's heart in the battlefield of life. We are truly grateful to God that the Muslim women of our nation have shown such skill in this regard.

Gender Regulations in Islam

"Wandering eyes will lead to a wandering heart." What does a wandering heart mean? It means a heart that cannot maintain love in a healthy and proper manner; it is a heart in which love continuously enters and leaves. This is what is meant by a wandering heart, and there is no shortage of individuals with such hearts. In novels, films, and on the news, you come across the lives of those who live in societies devoid of religion or belief. Both men and women place themselves in a potpourri of passionate situations outside of marriage which they call 'love'—this is not love, it is but a fleeting passion.

What is the outcome of such relationships? The outcome is that the essential centre of love—i.e., the family—loses its warmth, and rather than feeling care and affection for one another, the husband and wife become cold, indifferent, and inattentive to one another.

"Wandering eyes will lead to a wandering heart." When the heart begins to wander, human behaviour and interaction also begin to veer off from the straight path. Corruption, indecency, sensuality, hardship, adversity, and volatile situations, all stem from a wandering heart. So how can we protect ourselves from this wandering heart? By controlling the small apertures that we call 'eyes' and by controlling the small entrée that we call the 'tongue'.

فَلَا تَخْضَعْنَ بِالقَوْلِ فَيَطْمَعَ الَّذِي فِي قَلْبِهِ مَرَضٌ

... do not be complaisant in your speech, lest he in whose heart is a sickness should desire ... (33:32)

This verse counsels women that in their conversations with other men, they should not speak in a way that would cause a sick-hearted man—i.e., one who has a wandering heart—to begin to yearn for her.

There are some individuals who believe that Islam's proscriptions such as "cover yourselves" and "do not gaze at others," are nothing but a set of outdated rules. Recently, there have been some ranters who seem to affix the word 'outdated' to everything, as though this is the proper way to use it. These proscriptions in Islam are actually very precise and it behoves us to contemplate over them. Without contemplation, we cannot understand them. As Hafiz says:

When you hear the speech of the lovers (*ahl-i dil*) do not say it is mistaken / for the real mistake, my dear, is that you do not fathom their speech

These ranters do not fathom the depth and inner meaning of the proscriptions in Islam; yet they still insist on offering their own self-conjectured opinions!

Islam has prescribed certain things for men and certain things for women, and each of them are there to help build the inner family environment. The issue of observing the proper boundaries between men and women, the issue of covering oneself, the issue of not adorning oneself in front of unrelated men ... these are all intended to preserve the well-being of the family.

There are people who claim that Islam is a harsh and unbending religion, depriving men and women of natural pleasures. If we were to follow this same logic, then we would say the same about our intellects—i.e., they deprive man from many natural pleasures. For example, if your body is incapable of having sweet or oily foods, you are going to abstain from them no matter how delicious they may be or how much you crave them. Similarly, no matter how pleasant a drink may be, you would never consume it if it contained poison. You may have a craving for it, but your intellect tells you otherwise. It is the same with these proscriptions in Islam—observing the boundary between men and women, gender segregation, and other such rules within the sacred law all assist in preserving the inner family environment.

I constantly advise young men and women who are about to get married to keep a few things in mind. I advise the women not to do anything to make their husband jealous, and I also advise the men not to do anything to make their wives jealous. Women must be careful of how they behave at work, at school, or even with family and friends, so as not to arouse their husband's jealousy or suspicion. Likewise, men should also be careful of how they behave in these situations whether at work or at school. Both men and women should exercise caution when it comes to sweet-talking, conversing, joking, or laughing with the opposite gender. What Islam has prohibited has a direct bearing on the family.

If the seed of suspicion is planted, regardless of whether it is accurate or not, it will still have a negative effect. It is like a bullet that leaves a barrel; if it strikes a person's chest, it will kill him whether the shooter shot him intentionally or whether he pulled the trigger by accident. A bullet does not differentiate—it will not say, "since the person who pulled the trigger did so accidentally, I will not strike the target." It will strike the target. In the same way, harbouring suspicion will have its effect as well, regardless of whether it is based on the truth or whether it is based on imagination and misconstrued assumptions.

When a man and a woman are told to be careful of their gaze, when a woman is told not to beautify herself for other than her husband, when a man is told not to gaze at the adorned face of other than his wife, and when both are told to abstain from intermingling and having harmful interactions with the opposite gender, the primary reason for this is so that the inner family ambience can become one of safety and security, where the husband and wife can have an exclusive relationship. A husband and wife who both observe these limits will become cordially closer to each other. When this cordial relationship is strengthened, the family ambience is permeated with love and joy. This is why you see that in religious families, where both the husband and wife observe these guidelines, they have been living with each other happily for many years. Their love for each other remains strong and ties their hearts together such that it becomes difficult for them to separate. It is this kind of love and affection that makes the family endure and that is why Islam places such great importance on it.

The Worth of a Muslim Woman

It is sad to see some women today, pursuing a lifestyle of worthless excess whether it be the latest fashion, excessive makeup, ostentation, or the desire to compete with one another in acquiring a particular brand of clothing or appliance. A Muslim woman is far too noble to be preoccupied with such trivial matters. The status of a Muslim woman is much greater than to become victim to this consumeristic mentality. I am not saying these things are forbidden in Islam. What I am saying is that it is undignified for a Muslim woman to go in pursuit of gold, jewellery, and an array of household items or to be extravagant in her wants and desires at a time when so many people in our society are in need of assistance. Extravagance is not the path of a Muslim woman.

From time to time, I hear of some of the things that are occurring in society: dressing a certain way because it happens to be in vogue, wearing jewellery in a particular manner, replacing household items—or in colloquial speech "the décor of your home"—all at a great expense. This is not a source of pride. A woman's value is not based on wearing the latest fashion or walking in style (apparently some women even simulate their gait based on the European style). These are erroneous beliefs and illusions. The idea that just because a certain woman puts on airs and walks into a gathering in a particular outfit and hair-style, that we should now feel inferior to her and, hence, exert all our effort and spend all we can in order to match her style is simply outrageous. Do not ever feel inferior to such a person. Any individual who abases a woman because of her "unfashionable" clothing or "unstylish" taste in cosmetics, or because she does not have any gold around her wrist or neck, has really only abased himself. These are not the criteria of abasement. The greatest women on earth are not those whose sense of fashion or makeup is the one promoted by all the BurdaStyle fashion magazines of the world. Apparently, the best cosmetics and clothing can be found on the faces and bodies of the mannequins that line the windows of European fashion stores. I ask you, do these things have any value? Do these poor, helpless mannequins, who are welded in place daylong, have any value? This type of cosmetic is worn by many of the actresses whose moral fibre is under question.

The greatest women in history are those who have displayed prudence, resolution, proper judgement, and humanity. There was a lady in one of the eastern countries, whose name I do not wish to mention. She was prime minister of her country and was considered a great personality. Prior to the Islamic revolution in Iran, she was prime minister and still held that position when I had become the president. This lady was one of the strongest and most prominent female politicians in the world, and yet she always dressed and appeared very simply. A woman's worth, as you can see, is not based on her appearance. So let her not waste time in rivalry and ostentation when it comes to clothing, makeup, décor, etc. since it will only harm herself, create difficulties for her spouse, and gain nothing in the eyes of God; if anything, her stature will diminish in His eyes.

There was a time when Iran was like this. Fashion was all that occupied women's lives. We lived through those days and with the blessings of God when the revolution began, we left that dark period behind. There was a time when if a handful of women came together, their main topic of conversation would be about which dress is prettier, which woman has a more fashionable outfit, who walks and talks with style, etc. The bulk of the conversation would pertain to these topics. Fortunately, it is not like this today and rightly so. Today, the value of a Muslim woman is much greater than for her to be consumed by these trivial matters.

My dear Muslims sisters, most of you are not like this

but unfortunately, there are some who have been afflicted with this manner of thought. You have set out on a journey and achieved much, but be vigilant not to let your hidden enemies persuade you to turn back halfway and squander all your struggles. From the very beginning of the Revolution until now, our enemies have wasted no effort in trying to misguide the youth of this great nation—the revolutionary youth, the post-revolutionary youth, and the youth of today like yourselves—by trying to occupy you with materialistic concerns at the expense of your Islamic and revolutionary values. Who must stand up to them with strength and firmness? Everyone! But initially, it is you, the young revolutionary men and women. Some individuals assume that because it has been a few decades since the Revolution, we no longer need to worry about these things. In fact, we need to worry now more so than ever before. Some may believe that we must use all the new things the world can offer so we do not fall behind, but this is a false assumption. As God says:

$$\text{ما عِندَكُم يَنفَدُ وَما عِندَ اللَّـهِ باقٍ}$$

That which is with you will be spent, but what is with Allah shall endure ... (Naḥl, 16:96)

It is God's reward that is important and eternal. We need to strive for this, for it is what truly matters.

The Role of a Mother

The reason that Islam places such importance on the role of the woman within her family is because of the influence she can have on future generations. If a woman is dedicated and committed to her family, gives importance to raising the children, attends to them, feeds them, raises them by her side, and nourishes their minds at every opportune moment in the same way that she nourishes their bodies—through stories, religious training, narratives from the Qur'ān, instructional anecdotes, etc.—the future generations of that society will consist of a mature and thriving people. A mother can bring up her children in the best way possible. The way she trains her child is very different from what happens in a classroom; it is through her conduct, her conversations, her love, her cajoling, and even her lullabies—in short, it is through how she lives—that her child is trained. The more pious and wise the mother, the better the upbringing of the child will be.

A mother's role begins from the start of pregnancy and continues for the rest of that individual's life. A child who has grown into a youth or even an adult can still be influenced by his mother's love and affection, and her particular maternal ways. If our women could raise their level of education and understanding, the influence that they can have on a person is incomparable to the influence of any other cultural or ethical body. It is true that an uneducated mother may not have a significant [educational] effect on her child during his later years, but this is simply because she lacks that education; it is not because a mother is not influential. It is the mother, whether she knows it or not, that imparts the society's culture, education, and morality through her body, her soul, her character, and her conduct. Everyone is influenced by their mothers. If anyone ever reaches heaven, the first step towards it was with the foot of his mother:

الجنّة تحت أقدام الامّهات

Heaven lies beneath the feet of your mother.[16]

We need to teach our children to kiss their mother's hands; this is what Islam encourages. This can still be witnessed in those families that are more religious, more ethical, and closer to the principles of the faith. Children need to learn to respect their mother at home. This showing of respect does not oppose the warm, emotional relationship that exists between a mother and her children but it needs to be there.

The lady of the house must be respected, even if she never becomes a mother. A woman who is not thinking about having children or cannot have children is still a wife and we should never underestimate the role of a wife. If a man is to be useful in society, there must be a good woman at home; there is no other way.

A Muslim woman must strive towards education, spirituality, and self-refinement. She needs to be at the forefront of every struggle, regardless of what kind it is. She should pay no heed to shallow worldly glamour, but focus on maintaining her modesty and purity, which would naturally repel the unwanted gaze of strangers. She should be a reposing heart for her husband and children, and the source of peace and tranquillity within the family environment. In her tender, affectionate arms and with words of loving wisdom, she should raise children with healthy personalities—those who are full of vigour, psychologically robust, and free from emotional disorders. These will become the great men and women of tomorrow.

---

[9] *Nahj al-faṣāḥah*, ḥadīth no. 1328.

A mother is more valuable and more influential than any other instructive agency. It is possible for scientists to devise extremely sophisticated electronic devices, to build intercontinental missiles, and to invent means of conquering space ... but all of these inventions pale in comparison to the one who can give rise to a noble human being, and that is a mother. This is the paradigm for every Muslim woman.

The Rewarded Struggle of a Woman

It has been said that a woman's *jihād* is to be a good wife to her husband (*ḥusn al-tabaʿʿul*).[17] But what does being a good wife mean? Under the tyranny of the Shah, when I and others like me were working against the regime, sooner or later, they would identify us and send their people after us. They would come and forcefully take us from our homes, right in front of the eyes of our wives and children, and lock us up in the Savak prisons and torture chambers. I was able to tolerate the imprisonment; I was able to bear the torture; but all along, I knew that my wife was suffering more than I was. The worry, the fear, the sorrow, and the angst did not give her a moment's rest, and I knew this. Even when I was in solitary confinement, I knew that my family was suffering more than I was, and my heart went out to them.

When I was released and I attempted to inquire about their situation, even though they did not want to reveal anything to me, I could tell what they had to endure. Being all alone without a husband; looking after and providing for several young children, with no income, no savings, no

---

[17] *Al-Kāfī*, "Kitāb al-jihād, bāb jihād al-rajul wa al-marʾah."

means of comfort, and no security; being taunted by others; not knowing what condition the father of your children is in; this is real hardship and they had to bear it.

Some women would come and visit their husbands in prison. When the husband would ask, "How are things?" the wife would respond, "Everything is fine." The husband would ask, "Are you okay for money?" and she would say, "Yes, of course." He would ask, "Are the kids okay; why did you not bring them?" and she would respond, "They were busy playing and I did not want to interrupt them." Later, he would find out that the child was upset for a whole month, but the wife did not want her imprisoned husband to get worried. The husband would ask, "How about yourself? How are you coping?" And the wife would say, "I am doing quite well," even though she herself needed to be looked after. We had women like this and they were a strong support.

Of course, there were others who were not like this. As soon as they came to visit, they began complaining to their husbands of their difficulties: "You are not there ... we have no funds ... we have no food ... we have no support ... the children need their father ... the school is saying this about us ..." The poor man who already had a hundred worries of his own, now found his own determination fading away as a result. If he did not immediately begin writing his letter of contrition to the Shah in order to get out of prison, he would have surely been unable to keep his resolve for the next opportunity of resistance against the regime.

From the very beginning of the Islamic Revolution, women played a vital role in supporting it. Both during the Revolution as well as the momentous eight years of the Sacred Defence,[18] the role played by wives and mothers was no less important than that of the soldiers themselves; if anything, they actually bore a heavier, more painful, and more taxing burden. A mother who had raised her own dear son, the light of her eyes, for eighteen years or more until he had reached the peak of his upbringing through her motherly love, is now sending this young man towards the battlefield, not knowing whether his body will ever return. Can there be a comparison between her sacrifice and that of her son? Yes, this young man is going to war with faith, revolutionary spirit, and passion, but what his mother is doing is no less than him. Later, when they bring back his body, the mother takes pride in her martyred son. These are not small matters. This movement of women, the Zaynab-like movement, was a strong part of our revolution.

When our children catch a common cold or start coughing a bit, we begin to worry. Imagine now, a child who goes to the warfront and is killed; then a second goes and is killed; then a third goes and is killed; this not a trivial matter. Now, when a woman, with all that healthy, active, and energetic motherly affection, plays her role such that hundreds of other mothers find the strength and faith to send their own children to the warfront, you see the results of it. If at the time that their sons were heading for battle or when their bodies were brought back to them, they chose to lament and wail, to complain and protest at Imam Khomeini or at the war, then surely we would have lost the war within the first few years. This is the role the mothers of the martyrs played.

---

[18] *Difāʿ-I Muqaddas* (lit. 'Sacred Defence') refers to the Iran-Iraq War from 1980 to 1988.

We cannot forget the patient widows of the martyrs—those young women who had just started their sweet family lives. They gave up all the hopes that they had built for their marriage. Not only were they content for their young husbands to go to a place where they may not return and to bear their martyrdom, but they took pride in this with their heads raised high. These are the priceless roles that they played.

And finally, to this day, there are women who marry those veterans wounded on the battlefield; they offer their lives to help and support men who are scarred—both physically and mentally—by the trauma of war. Out of their own free will, without any coercion, they decide to take responsibility for looking after such veterans. This is called sacrifice. It is one thing to commit a few hours a day to look after someone, in which case, at the end of the day, you can return home with a note of gratitude. It is quite another thing when you decide to marry the person and live in his house all day long. He is forever indebted to you. This is what was required, and these women sacrificed themselves for it. There is absolutely no way to quantify the role that these women played. And I will state and admit that the first person to understand this role that women played was our great leader, Imam Khomeini (r).

My sisters, know that all of the difficulties you endure on account of your husbands' duties are not wasted in the least. Settle your accounts with God, ask Him for your payment, and know that He will surely reward you. I have always said that in these types of affairs, the rewards that women will receive in the Hereafter will make up *at least* half of all the rewards given out. They often ask me why I say "at least"; after all, justice dictates that the reward is split evenly between men and women. So why should women potentially receive more? I respond to them in this manner: when a man does something, it is out there in public for everyone to see; hence, he receives praise and commendation from the people, and this is a part of his reward. But a woman who is working behind the scenes is unappreciated because no can see what she has to bear; she receives no applause, commendation, or laurels, and this is why her reward is greater.

When a wife at home is in agreement with what her husband is doing, the husband's potential to act and strive increases several fold. If a man strives in any arena, it is largely because of his wife's cooperation, support, patience, and accommodating attitude. It has always been this way. Hence, when the Prophet (ṣ) said that a woman's *jihād* is being a good wife, this is what being a good wife means—i.e., to prepare the grounds so that her husband can perform his duties. Some people think that a woman's *jihād* is only to provide comfort for her husband, but this is not what being a good wife only means. This is not *jihād*. *Jihād* is when a believing and self-sacrificing woman agrees to carry part of her husband's burden at a time when he has been tasked with a heavy responsibility. When a man becomes weary, this becomes manifest in the home environment; when he returns home, he may appear tired, frustrated, and in a bad mood. This bad mood could be transferred to the home from outside. Now if his wife wants to perform *jihad*, then her *jihad* is to be patient with these difficulties and to bear them for the sake of God. This is being a good wife.

When the Prophet of Islam (ṣ) emigrated from Makkah to Madinah, Imam ʿAlī (ʿa) was around twenty-three or twenty-four years old. This was about the same time that all the different battles began. In all of these battles, this young man was either the standard-bearer, the commander, or the main combatant. In short, he bore most of the responsibilities of war on his shoulders, and war never pays heed to time. It cares not if the weather is too hot or too cold, if the time is too early or too late, if your son is sick or not. In the ten years of the Prophet's (ṣ) rule, there were about seventy major and minor military campaigns. Some lasted for only a few days, while others lasted for months. Imam ʿAlī (ʿa) was present in all except one. On top of these battles, he would also be sent on assignments by the Prophet (ṣ), such as the assignment to Yemen, where the Prophet (ṣ) appointed him as a judge for a short period of time. Therefore, Lady Fāṭimah (ʿa) was always faced with either her husband being away at war, returning with a wounded body, being occupied with matters in the city of Madinah with the Prophet (ṣ) or away on an assignment. Yet, in this difficult situation and with a husband who was always labouring away, Lady Fāṭimah (ʿa) continued her work with the utmost patience and kindness. She raised four children under her own heavenly supervision, including Ḥusayn ibn ʿAlī (ʿa). In all the history of mankind to the present day, you cannot find any flag of freedom and dignity raised higher than the one raised by her son, Ḥusayn (ʿa). This is the meaning of being a good wife.

CLOSING WORDS OF ADVICE

Key Advice to Women

My dear sisters, if you ever have to face hardship on account of the work and struggles of your husbands, know that God will reward you for it even if no one ever finds out what you endure for a moment. Many men are not aware of what a woman must bear; they think that hardship pertains to physical struggle but they are oblivious of the fact that emotional and spiritual hardships are sometimes more difficult to bear. Men may not fully grasp much of what you go through, but God is He *"from whom no hidden thing is hidden."*[19] He watches over you and your reward is secured with Him. Hence, the more you contribute to the success of

---

[19] *Al-Kāfi*, "al-Rawḍah, Khuṭbah li Amīr al-muʾminīn."

the young man by your side who has this responsibility, the more you will increase your reward, value, and status next to God.

In fact, your reward is guaranteed more than that of your husband's. This is because if your husband does a good deed not for the sake of God—i.e., out of ostentation (*riyā*), God forbid, or any other inappropriate reason—he will lose his reward. In contrast, when you look after him, nurture the children, protect his trust and honour, preserve his reputation, pave the ways of comfort, approach him with a smile, and live with him as an honourable wife, your reward is guaranteed. This is a great distinction.

If your husband is in the field of studies or is active in the affairs of the Islamic Republic, you should work with him so that he can perform his duties with ease. Any person who works for God, his spouse is doing the same as well. Value the work of such individuals. They are amongst the best people of our country today. Why? Because when you see a society that is solely concerned with personal gain and will do anything to achieve this end—through lying, committing fraud, flattery, distorting the truth, oscillating between this group and that, uttering words to win the hearts of the unjust, and other such schemes which are undoubtedly much worse outside of our country—you can find individuals who, despite living in such conditions, still choose professions that aid them to fulfil their duties. Such an individual and profession are both honourable, particularly when the task is difficult or dangerous. To be married to an individual like this is a source of pride.

My sisters, appreciate these men, these jobs and even

the difficulties these jobs bring. You should know that it is men such as these who wipe the filth of dependence, corruption, and humiliation from the face of a nation. Any nation with men who are ready to take on responsibilities and risk their lives is able to manage its own affairs. In contrast, a nation that is inclined to seek shelter under the shade of ease even at the expense of pushing out hundreds of people from that shade—i.e., a nation that lacks self-sacrificial, combatant, brave, informed, and decisive men on the path of truth—will never be able to escape humiliation even after centuries. The distress that they managed to bring down upon our nation for a period of time is exactly the same distress that they are bringing down today upon so many of the Muslim and non-Muslim nations of the world.

So be proud of your menfolk since their efforts are dear in the eyes of God. Assisting them and being on the same path as them should be a source of pride for you. With the right intention, whatever you offer such a man—who is your husband and is spending his youth in the way of God—you are offering to God. Your married life is not just a simple life of marriage; it is a life of service. So have hope in divine reward and value this opportunity which you have been granted.

You are like my own daughters and sisters, and your husbands are like my own sons. Spouses like you are a source of pride. But know that people will be observing you as well. If they see that someone's wife is devoting too much attention to beautification, ornamentation, ostentation, and other meaningless endeavours, they will say, "Look at those who make all these claims; this is how their wives are." Hence, you must be very attentive. To protect your husband's reputation is actually to protect the reputation of the Revolution and the reputation of the entire nation; you must protect it.

Families such as these have some privileges and some limitations; it is the same everywhere and everyone is like this. You cannot always have everything you want. One must be patient; one must live in a way that God is pleased with. I cannot overemphasize this to you: pay attention to religious and revolutionary values, be exemplars of the Revolution, and become paragons of a revolutionary woman. Do not give into luxury and lavishness. Let it not be that whatever you earn is spent in attaining gold and jewellery; this is beneath your honour.

God addresses the wives of the Prophet (ṣ) in the Qurʾān:

$$يا نِساءَ النَّبِيِّ مَن يَأتِ مِنكُنَّ بِفاحِشَةٍ مُبَيِّنَةٍ يُضاعَف لَهَا العَذابُ ضِعفَينِ وَكانَ ذٰلِكَ عَلَى اللَّـهِ يَسيرًا$$

O wives of the Prophet! Whoever of you commits a gross indecency, her punishment shall be doubled, and that is easy for Allah. (Aḥzāb 33:30)

Why is their punishment doubled if they commit a sin? It is because they are the wives of the Prophet. The opposite is also true:

$$وَمَن يَقنُت مِنكُنَّ لِلَّـهِ وَرَسولِهِ وَتَعمَل صالِحًا نُؤتِها أَجرَها مَرَّتَينِ وَأَعتَدنا لَها رِزقًا كَريمًا$$

But whoever of you is obedient to Allah and His Apostle

*and acts righteously, We shall give her a twofold reward,
and We will have in store for her a noble provision.
(Aḥzāb 33:31)*

Any worship or good deed that they perform will be rewarded
twofold. In other words, the reward for the prayer of the wife
of the Prophet (ṣ) is generally twice that of another person;
but if, God forbid, she were to backbite another person, it
would count doubly against her.

يا نِساءَ النَّبِيِّ لَستُنَّ كَأَحَدٍ مِنَ النِّساءِ إِنِ اتَّقَيتُنَّ

*O wives of the Prophet! You are not like other women if
you are wary [of Allah] ... (Aḥzāb 33:32)*

In other words, if you observe God-wariness (*taqwā*) you will
have a distinction over other women. Immediately, the verse
continues:

فَلا تَخضَعنَ بِالقَولِ فَيَطمَعَ الَّذي في قَلبِهِ مَرَضٌ
وَقُلنَ قَولًا مَعروفًا

*... do not be complaisant in your speech, lest he in whose
heart is a sickness should aspire and speak honourable
words. (Aḥzāb 33:32)*

Even though these verses are addressed to the Prophet's
wives, the verses are not exclusive to them. They can be
applied to anyone who is connected to the Prophet (ṣ).

Key Advice to Men

I must also tell you young men that you should be immaculate when it comes to looking after your wives. A man of faith—a man who works for God—must ensure that all aspects of his life are Godly. One such aspect of life is interacting with your family, especially your wife and children. You must be a paragon of virtues. At times, some small incident outside of the house may make you angry, but this anger should never show itself when you come home. Be kind to your wives. Be a father, in the true sense of the word, for your children. On various occasions, I have always told people in positions of responsibility to be a father to their children and not a stranger to them.

Attend to your family. Do not say that you bear heavy responsibilities on your shoulders. Do not think that leaving work an hour or two later and coming home without a smile is not a big deal and the sky will not come crashing down. I have spoken about this to the administrators in our country. I say that you must set aside a few hours of your day and some of your free time and dedicate it to your family. Give your wife and children your love, affection, consideration, and attention. Do not neglect your home and family life. Some people leave their house first thing in the morning and do not come back until late at night. This is not right. To those who can, we recommend even going home to your wife and children for lunch. Eat your lunch with your family, spend some time together, and then go back to work. At a suitable time in the evening after work, return home, see the children, and spend some quality time with your family. It should not be the case that a woman feels that by marrying a man of responsibility, there will no longer be any peace or comfort in her life. This is not how it should be. For you and I who shoulder responsibility, our love, affection, and attention towards our family should be greater than that of the average person. You must become paragons in this regard.

Today, your children are in need of a kiln of love and that is the family structure. Attend to your children and deal with them as a father and friend. The best fathers are those who are friends with their sons and daughters. On the one hand, they offer their fatherly authority and guidance and a helping and loving hand, but on the other, they also offer the intimacy of a friend. If your child has a question, or wants to talk, or needs to confide in someone, let it be to you or your wife that he first turns to.

My dear young men, my fatherly advice to you is to structure your interactions within your family wisely. What does this mean? It means to be kind, to be present in the house to the extent possible, to be intimate with one's family, and to attend to their needs; it is to refrain from being neglectful and ill natured. Today, this great responsibility is for you to bear. Your children are like seedlings whose roots are connected to yours; it is up to you to support them, keep them secure, and let them feel they have a warm support to rely upon.

Spend time with your children and interact with them; work with your wife and be kind to her. Your wife should truly feel that you appreciate all the hard work she does. If you had a wife who did not support you or work with you, you would have had a difficult time with your tasks. Try it out. Ask your wife to deal with you inconsiderately and you will see how difficult it can be. The fact that she works with you, assists you, has a pleasant disposition, takes care of the house, looks after the children, and preserves the serenity of the home is one of the biggest reasons for your success. Many men who go out to the public sphere—whether it be politics, business, military, or any other arena of work—and return home tired after a hard day of work, seem to assume that they have performed this incredible feat while their wives have been sitting idle behind the front lines. They are largely ignorant of the fact that had their wives not been behind the front lines, they themselves would not have been able to do anything on the "battlefield". Appreciate your wives. May there never be a man of faith in support of the Revolution who acts against the Islamic teachings on how a man should treat his wife. Of course, I do not mean to suggest that women are infallible and the men are always to blame. Women must also cooperate, be of assistance, and endure the hardships since such hardships will always exist.

This is my advice to you young men and women, fathers and mothers. Let not this advice enter one ear and exit from the other. Preserve them in your mind for they were spoken with all seriousness. I would be pleased if I knew that this advice was followed with utmost attention.

We hope that God Almighty, through the blessings of Lady Fāṭimah (ʿa) and Imam ʿAlī (ʿa)—who truly are the paragons of marriage in all that we have said—grants you success and sanctifies your life. May God assist you in having a sweet and felicitous life and may He endow you with the tranquillity that He has promised to people in marriage.

GLOSSARY

ākhirah	The Afterlife.
ʿalayhi al-salām	An expression that means "peace be upon him"; It appears after the name of one of the Infallibles and is abbreviated as (ʿa) in the text.
ʿazab (pl. *ʿuzzāb*)	Unmarried man or woman.
chādor	An Iranian form of *ḥijāb* for women.
dunyā	This world.
fiṭrah	Man's God-given innate disposition.
ḥadīth	Narration from the Prophet (ṣ) or one of the Infallibles.
ḥijāb	Covering, veil.
jāhilī	Ignorant, mindless; a practice which resembles the crude pre-Islamic age (*Jāhiliyyah*).
jihād	Struggle and effort in the path of God.
kalimah ṭayyibah	Good word.
mahr al-sunnah	The customary modest dowry established by the Prophet (ṣ).

maḥram	Sacred; close relative or being in a degree of consanguinity precluding marriage.
maʿṣūmīn	Infallibles—the term can include the previous prophets, the Noble Prophet (ṣ), his daughter Fāṭimah (ʿa), and the Imams from his family.
qahramān	Housekeeper, foreman.
qawām	Upright, stature, strength, support.
raḥmatullah ʿalayhī	An expression that means "May God's mercy be upon him"; It is often used after mention of the names of the saints and scholars of Islam.
rayḥān	Sweet-smelling plant; blossom; bounty.
riyā	Ostentation.
sakan	Abode of rest and repose.
sakana	To dwell; to take rest; to be tranquil; to take comfort.
ṣallallahu ʿalayhī wa ālihi wa sallama	An expression that means "may God salute and send peace on him and his family"; It appears after the name of the Holy Prophet and is abbreviated as (ṣ) in the text.

sunnah	Precedent; way of life; The practice and custom of the Prophet (ṣ) and his noble family.
taqwā	God-consciousness, God-wariness, piety.
walīmah	Customary feast due to marriage or birth.
zawj	Pair, couple; husband, wife.

INDEX OF QURʾĀNIC VERSES

16:53	Whatever blessing you have is from Allah, and when a distress befalls you, you make entreaties to Him.	25
16:80	It is Allah who has made your homes as a place of rest (*sakan*) for you ...	38
16:96	That which is with you will be spent, but what is with Allah shall endure ...	115
24:32	... If they are poor, Allah will enrich them out of His grace ...	13
30:21	And of His signs is that He created for you spouses from among yourselves so that you may find rest in them, and He put between you love and compassion; most surely there are signs in this for a people who reflect.	14, 37
33:30	O wives of the Prophet! Whoever of you commits a gross indecency, her punishment shall be doubled, and that is easy for Allah.	128
33:31	But whoever of you is obedient to Allah and His Apostle and acts righteously, We shall give her a twofold reward, and We will have in store for her a noble provision.	129

33:32	... do not be complaisant in your speech, lest he in whose heart is a sickness should desire ...	109, 129
33:35	Indeed the Muslim men and the Muslim women, the faithful men and the faithful women ... Allah holds in store for them forgiveness and a great reward.	81
37:61	Let all workers work for the like of this!	58
66:10-12	Allah cites an example of the faithless: the wife of Noah and the wife of Lot. They were under two of our righteous servants, yet they betrayed them ... And Mary, daughter of Imran, who guarded the chastity of her womb, so We breathed into it of Our spirit. She confirmed the words of her Lord and His Books, and she was one of the obedient.	102
103:3	and enjoin one another to [follow] the truth, and enjoin one another to patience.	61

NOTES